# PORT ARRIVALS AND IMMIGRANTS TO THE CITY OF BOSTON

# PORT ARRIVALS AND IMMIGRANTS TO THE CITY OF BOSTON

1715-1716
and
1762-1769

Compiled Under the Direction of
WILLIAM H. WHITMORE

With a Reconstructed Index

Excerpted and Reprinted From
*A Volume of Records Relating to the Early History of Boston Containing Miscellaneous Papers*
Registry Department of the City of Boston
29th in the series formerly called *Record Commissioners' Reports*
Document Number 100
Boston, 1900

Reprinted with a Reconstructed Index and Re-paged
Genealogical Publishing Co., Inc.
Baltimore, 1973

*Library of Congress Cataloging in Publication Data*
Main entry under title:
Port arrivals and immigrants to the city of Boston, 1715-1716 and 1762-1769.
An excerpt (p. 229-317 inclusive) from A volume of records relating to the early history of Boston containing miscellaneous papers, prepared by the Registry Dept. of Boston, and published in 1900.
1. Boston—Genealogy. 2. Ship registers—Boston. I. Whitmore, William Henry, 1836-1900. II. Boston. Registry Dept. A volume of records relating to the early history of Boston containing miscellaneous papers.
F73.25.P67 929'.3744'61 72-10875
ISBN 0-8063-0541-X

Reprinted for
Clearfield Company, Inc. by
Genealogical Publishing Co., Inc.
Baltimore, Maryland
1989, 1996

Vessells Entered in y^e month of January 1714/5

Jan. 3 John Rayner y^e Sloop Friends Adventure from Surrenam
No Passengers
11 John Hambly y^e Sloop Newport from Rhoad Island
No Passengers
Stephen Toman y^e Sloop Elizabeth from Surrenam
Kelly A Taylor

Vessells Entered in y^e Month of Febuary: 1714/5

Feb. 16 Abrah^a Miller y^e Sloop Mary from Anopalis
No Passengers
Nath^a. Fadre y^e Sloop.
24 Edward Smith y^e Barke Adventure from Maryland
No Passengers
26 Joseph Gorham y^e sloop Increas from Connecticott
No Passengers
28 Thom^s. Bell y^e sloop Mary from Maryland
No Passengers
Tho^s. Lathrop y^e Sloop Adventure from Philadephia
Elis^a. Parrih. W^m M^cCoy A mercht.
28 James Coden y^e Sloop Mary from (Rhoad Island) N: Yorke
No Passengers
Moses Abbott y^e Sloop Pellican from Maryland
No Passengers
Francis Vandike y^e Sloop Tryall from New York.
No Passengers

Vessells Entered in y^e month of March 1715.

Mar. 1 Jacob Boardman y^e Sloop Elizabeth from North Carolina
No Passengers.
Ebenezr Chamberlain y^e Sloop Martha from ditto
No Passengers
2 James Duncan y^e sloop Swan from Virginia
No Passengers.
9 Francis Norris y^e Brig^t. Martha from Mountserat.
No Passengers but a Marriner.
17 John Braddick y^e Sloop John & Mary from New London
Coll^o Joseph Whieam of South Hould
W^m Beekman y^e Sloop Speadwell from New-york
Cornelios Van-horne A Merch^t.
22 W^m Bill y^e Sloop Anna from Compeachey
John Williams & Charles Anderson. Laguners.

Mar. 23 Thom[s] Daggett y[e] Brig[t]. Leopard from new castle
No Passengers but Marriners.
Philip Kelinack y[e] Sloop John from Virginia
No Passengers
Dan[l]. Low y[e] sloop Two Brothers from North Carolina
No Passengers.
24 John Lovell y[e] Sloop Robert from Virginia
John Ward a Labourer
25 John Steel y[e] sloop Hope from Surrenam
No Passengers
Abiel Jones y[e] Brig[t] Mayflower from Barbados
Cap[t]. Tho[s]. Child
Joseph Clark y[e] ship Nathaniel from Compeachey
No Passengers.

Vessells Entered in y[e] month of March 1715/16.

Mar. 2 Rich[d]. Pitcher y[e] Snow W[m] & James from Isle of Thera
No Passengers.
Charles Howell y[e] Sloop Mary from North Carrolina
No Passengers
Robert Miers y[e] Brig[t]. Lamb from Campeachy
Thomas Naping a Bayman
3[d] Hugh Crage y[e] Sloop John from South Carolina
John Tate a Mercht.
5 Joseph Prince y[e] Sloop Seaflower from N. Carrolina
No Passengers.
6 Ebene[r] Chamberlin y[e] Sloop Martha from ditto.
No Passengers.
Thomas Lathrop y[e] Sloop Adventure from Virginia.
No Passengers
10 Isaac Perkins y[e] Sloop Unity from Maryland
Joseph Coates a marriner
12 Francis Norris y[e] Brigt Martha & Han[a]. from Mountserat
No Passengers
15 Thomas Bell y[e] Sloop Seaflower from Maryland
Henry Ballard A youth & three marriners
16 Thomas Fry y[e] Sloop Tryall from Antigua
Francis Ditty, John Dolle, marriners
23 David Jenkins y[e] Snow Betty from Fyall
No Passengers.
26 John Brett y[e] Sloop Adventure from Fyall
No Passengers
27 Will[m]. Levingstone y[e] Ship Neptune from Surrenam
Barshaba Hart a widdow, Rosamond Thom a spinster
28 John Mitchell y[e] Sloop Hana. & Mary from N. Carrolina
No Passengers.

Vessells entered in y^e month of May 1716.

May 2 Miles Rainsbotham y^e Sloop Jane & Mary from N: Carolina
No Passengers
3 Thomas Barber y^e Sloop Union from Long Island
No Passengers
Timothy Yeals y^e Sloop Two Friends from North Carolina
No Passengers
John Ford y^e Sloop Begining from New York.
Anthony Coignand A French man
John Mullins y^e Sloop Pellican from North Carolina
Ann Arrington a Spinster
James Nolan y^e Sloop Providence from North Carolina
Tho^s Cary Esq a gentleman
Jonathan Hart y^e Sloop John & Robert from Harb^r Island
No Passengers
4 John Horton y^e Sloop Hannah from South Carolina
Mary Phillips a widow & two children
Adoniram Collins y^e Sloop Speadwell from Connecticutt
No Passengers
Thomas Cathcart y^e Sloop Jane & Eliz^a. from North Carolina
No Passengers
James Manson y^e Skooner Mayflower from North Carolina
Thomas Parris A merch^t
Joseph Glover y^e Sloop Mary from North Carrolina
No Passengers but a Marriner.
5 Thomas Peck y^e Sloop Mary from Virginia
No Passengers.
7 Nich^o Davis y^e Sloop Sus^a. & Sarah from Surrenam
No Passengers.
Jere^ah Owen y^e Sloop Sarah from St. Christopers
John Fiffield A marriner
10. Edward Cruff y^e Sloop Daniel from Turk Island
No Passengers
Josiah Prince y^e Sloop May Flower from N. London
Phineas Lathrop A Taylor
11 Endigo Potter y^e Sloop Two Brothers from Maryland
No Passengers
Edmond Wilkinson y^e Sloop Abigail & Ruth from New London
No Passengers.
14 John White y^e Sloop Content from St Christophers
No Passengers
Thomas Curtis y^e Sloop Two Brothers from New London
Tho^s Lathrop y^e Sloop Adventure from Phillidelphia
Joseph Taylor a Planter

May Mrs Pumroy a widow
Eliza Parris
Francis Vandyke y^e Sloop Tryall from New York
No Passengers.
Mallachy Salter y^e Sloop Mary from North Carolina
No Passengers.
Nath^l Breed y^e Snow Amity from Glasgow
Elizabeth Campbell, Her mother & four Daughters
Thomas Young a Youth
William Kerkwood a Pedlar & Thirteen men servants
Tho^s Coverly y^e Sloop Bahama from Bahama
John Sutton a Housewright & seven marriners.
Edmond Freeman y^e Sloop Farmers Tryall from Connecticut
No Passengers
15 John Brooks y^e Sloop Seaflower from New York.
No Passengers
Thomas Cooper y^e Sloop Middleton from Connecticott
Mrs Bull & three children
Mary Jess a Widow
W^m Goff a Marriner
16 John Wakefield y^e Sloop Hope from North Carolina
No Passengers.
17 And^r Robinson y^e Brig Mary & Abigail from Madera
No Passengers
21 Tho^s Pensy y^e Ship W^m & Mary from Bristoll
Capt. Paul Portlock }
Capt. Rob^t. Welch } Marriners.
Capt. Tho^s Willoby }
Tho^s Sanders A Blacksmith.
Tho^s More a Shipwright
Jos^s Cearl a Cordwainer & Fourteen Marriners.
Tho^s Porter y^e Ship Strewberry from Surrenam
John Steevens a Merch^t.
Tho^s. Fleming y^e Sloop Grayhound from South Carolina
Tho^s Cuttler a Merch^t
W^m Loughton a Ditto.
Francis Britton a Planter.
John Jenkins y^e Brig^t Jer^a & Tho^s from Jamaica
No Passengers.
Phillip Kelineck y^e Sloop Dove from Virginia
No Passengers.
Robert Campbell y^e Ship Truth & Daylight from Ireland
John Williams a Joyner.
James Kelly a do.
Ellinor Williams & two children
Lewis Cary of New York
Rich^d How a Glover. Tho^s Swift a Shooemaker
Two Marriners & Eleven Male Servts. no Trades
Four Female Serv^ts

May 22 Ellis Husk y$^e$ Ship Riga from Lisbone
No Passengers
Arthur Reaks y$^e$ Ship Four Sisters from Lisbone
No Passengers.
Sam$^{ll}$. Waters y$^e$ Sloop Dolphin from Cape Fransway
No Passengers.
22 John Jones y$^e$ Ship Boston Merch$^{ts}$ from Bris[tol].
W$^m$ Vincent a Joyner
Tho$^s$ Attwood a Gentlem$^n$
W$^m$ Walter a Carpent$^r$ & his Wife
Henry Atkins a Sailmaker
W$^m$ Tayler a Seale Maker
Henry Hooper Chiug$^n$ & servts.
John Tilley & 8 serv$^{ts}$ a Ropemaker
Caleb Fisher a Weavor
Phillip Parmitor a Marriner
Benj$^a$ Bryant a Carpenter & Seven Servt$^s$
23 Will$^m$ Cradder y$^e$ Ship Hanover from London
Capt. Tho$^s$ Porter. Capt Sam$^{ll}$. Cary
Sam$^{ll}$. Banister Merch$^t$ Mad$^m$ Banister
24 Phillip Callender y$^e$ Sloop Mary form Rhoad Island
No Passengers.
Will$^m$ Gold y$^e$ Sloop Caulfield from Anapolis
Joseph — a Soulder
Thom$^s$ Chase y$^e$ sloop Vinyard from Connecticutt
Eph$^r$ Arnold a Marriner
Will$^m$ Walter y$^e$ Sloop Dolphin from Anapolis
Peter Presious a Soulder
Eliza Standburry a widdow
28 Thom$^s$ Clarke y$^e$ Sloop York from Antigua
Capt Tho$^s$ Staples
Capt Tho$^s$ Mousell
Cap$^t$ W$^m$ Bill
Thom$^s$ Vernam y$^e$ Ship Two Sistors from Barnstaple
Capt. James Rude & five marriners
Samuel Grubb a Youth
Thomas Gruble a Marriner
29 Rich$^d$ Langley y$^e$ ship Mary from London
No Passengers
Maverick Thomas y$^e$ Sloop Martha from North Carolina.
William Turell a Husbandman
Samuel Turrell ditto
Charles Denman Merch$^t$.
James Davis Bricklayer
31 Endymion Walker y$^e$ Ship Concord from Topsham
John Prince an Upholsterer
Will$^m$ Ridge a Youth
Timothy Astell y$^e$ ship Allen from London
William Allen Mercht$^s$ & three servts
Oxenbridge Thatcher Gent$^m$ & servant
Samuel Thaxter Ditto and serv$^t$

John Dassett shoemaker
William Brickhead upoulsterer
Sam[ll] Vickers a serv[t]
Rachal Richardson ditto several marriners
Sundry Vessells from Turtuda but no Passengers.

Vessells entered in the month of June 1716.

June 1 Robert Whetberby y[e] Ship Robert & Eliz[a] from Fegaria
No Passengers.
4 John Ellery the Ship Anne Gally from Marriland
William Grahor a Merch[t].
Jabez Crowell y[e] Sloop Fairfield from Connecticut
Tho[s]. Holland a Merch[t].
Dorithy Davis a Spinster
John Kent y[e] Sloop Neptune from St. Christophers
No Passengers
John Tabor y[e] Brigh[t] Hopewell from Tertuda
No Passengers
5 Joseph Gorham y[e] Sloop Increase from Connecticut
No Passengers
Thomas Chichester y[e] Bark Mary from St Christophers
Rich[d]. Pullen. Adam Leland a Mercht
William Pinsent Marriner.
Charles Deming the Brig[t] Swallow from Barbados
No Passengers.
6 Charles Hogg the Snow Dolphin from Barbados.
No Passengers
Tho[s] Gallop y[e] Ship Crown from Bristoll
Robert Sugett a Cooper
6 John Slocomb the Ship Eliza from London
Henry Caswell a Mercht
Benja. Edwards a Marriner
William Brooker y[e] Ship Restoration from London
Isaac Lopez Mercht
Abra[m] Gotatus ditto
Jacob Ruggles ditto.
8 William Lane y[e] Ship Loyall Heine from Fyall
No Passengers
John Pitts y[e] Ship John & Sarah from Barbados
Edward Cordwin Mercht.
9 Edward Burroughs y[e] Sloop Abigail from Connecticut
No Passengers
Danil Pulcifer y[e] Sloop Manchester from Mariland
No Passengers
Gersham Cobb y[e] Sloop Brothers Society from Connecticut
Aron Melish a Mercht.
11 Nicholas Fogwell y[e] Sloop Francis & Katharine from Barbados
William Brayde a Doctr.
John Blaize a Marriner.

Abraham Cornwell ye Brigtt. Anna from Barbados
John Ruggles, Marriner
Joseph Knapton a Joyner
Daniel Wycr ye Sloop Seaflower from Connecticut
John King a Marriner.
June 12 Luke Anderson ye Sloop St. Peter & St. Andrew from Barbados No Passengers
John Webster ye Sloop Tryall from Curretuck
No Passengers
14 Thomas Arnold the Sloop Judeth from Cape Fransway
No Passengers
John Codner ye Ship Martha from Tortuda
No Passengers
15 John Tallaway ye Ship Friendship from Barbados
No Passengers
18 John Reynor ye Sloop Friends Adventure from New-foundland
Thos Hall Robin Strange James Harris } all
John Porter Edwd Ashly. Edwd Hynes } Marriners
Robert Mackrell ye Ship Mary Ann from Dublin
John Gallard a Gentm & his waiting man
Thos Barber ye Sloop Fryall from Mariland
Andrew Woodbery Marriner.
John Pomrey ye Sloop Mary from Antigua
No Passengers.
19 John Ford ye Sloop Begining from New York
No Passengers
20 Richard Brown ye Sloop Virgins Venture from Jamaica
Sam Rogers a Doctor. John Macklin a Carpenter
Wm Spencer ye Sloop Pine Apple from St Christopher
Jonas Gretty [?] a Marriner
Saml Pompillion "
William Beckman ye Sloop Speadwell from New York
No Passengers
21 Joseph Sherbun ye Pink Sarah from Madera
No Passengers
William Punchard ye Sloop Endeavour from Long Island
Stephen Winston a Joyner
John Brown ye Ship Richd & John from London
Benja Woodbridge a Marriner
Powell Howard a ditto
22 William Dove ye Brigtt Success from Jamaica
No Passengers.
23 Saml Raymond ye Sloop Deborah from South Carolina
No Passengers
Nehemiah Doan ye Sloop Rebecca from Connecticut
One Marriner
25 William Bleay ye Sloop Hannah & Mary from Compeachy
No Passengers

June 25 Peter Johnson ye Brig[tt] Adventure from Marriland
No Passengers
John Rawlings ye Ship Mayflower from Cape Fransway
No Passengers
George Woodhouse ye Ship Success from Hull & Fyall
John Belligner
Nich[l] Oursell ye Ship Globe from Ireland
John Bedford, Charles Obara Shoe Makers
James Hines, Cooper
W[m] Ennis, Peirce Shortell, Carpenters
John Edward, Tho[s] Lindly, Smiths
John & Benj[a] Wilcock Lock-Smiths
John Ennis, Currier
Henry Coulton, Printer
Thomas Baxter, Naylor
W[m] Baxter ditto
Chris[t] Pescot, Pattoon Maker
Abra[m] Barnes Silver & Gold Cup Maker
Daniel Gibbs, Silver Smith
Robert Darky, Taylor
Barb[y] Bradford Katherine Wittehead, Lace Makers.
Eliza Doyle, Coock
Mary Reed, Milener
Mary Crompston, Ribon Weaver
Mary Antwisdal, Button Maker
Mary Grant, Bedcase weaver. Mary Horne, East[a]: Potts. Ma[m] Jane Damby, Coock
Maite John & Patrick fargison Marriners

26 Joshua Thomas the Sloop Union from Barbados
No Passengers.
Nath[l] Uring, ye Ship Princes of Portingal from Madera
James Clark a Merchant.

27 Henry Foster ye Ship Sedgewick from ye Isle of May
No Passengers
William Alden ye Sloop Speadwell from Annapolis
Tho[s] Wetherbe a Souldier.
Joseph Prince ye Sloop Seaflower from North Carolina
No Passengers.
Jacob Boardman ye Sloop Eliza. from North Carolina
Benj[a] Edey a Carpenter & one Marriner.

27 Henry Davis ye Brigg[t] Speadwell from Antigua
John Drew a Taylor

28 John Braddick ye Sloop Revenge from New London
Hanah Goodale Spinster

29 Tho[s] Lathrop ye Sloop Adventure from New London
No Passengers

30 Abraham Howard ye Ship Brittania from Barbados
Benj[a] Woodbridge a Youth
William —— a servant
John Osborn ye Ship Patience & Judith from London
Adam Woods Woolcomber

Andrew Forbes Merch[t]
Mark Hading a Joyner & his wife
Patrick Ogilve Merch[t]
Jos[h] Brandon a Serv[t] to W[m] Allen
Tho[s]. Tims Merch[t]

| | |
|---|---|
| Tho[s] Dresser, John Kimball, Redmon Johnin, James Hyde, Tho[s]. Sherbon, Tho[s] Wincall John Fitygerrill, Tho[s] Foster, Jos[h] Green Story King & William Symonds. | All Marriners. |

These are to Acquaint the Select men of Boston, that I John Bell living in King Street Boston, have lett out a small part of my Shop to John Hall watchmaker; who came from London about 5 months agoe as I am informed; a single person and of a sober life & conversation and follows his business very dilligently; I took him into my Shop upon Thursday the 29[th] day of March last past: 1716

from yours to serve.

John Bell

Boston July 30[th] 1716

Lately arrivd from London. Francis Dewing who Engraveth and Printeth Copper Plates, Likewise Coats of Arms and Cyphers on Silver Plate. He Likewise Cuts Neatly in wood and Printeth Callicoes. &c.

Lodging at M[rs] Hawksworths against the Bunch of Grapes in King Street arrivd in the Jollif Galley capt Aram Commander the begining of July 1716.

Massachusetts Impost Office. Boston.

Vessels Entered in the month of July 1716.

July 2 Benj[a] Shommedieu y[e] Sloop Ann from New London
No Passengers
Tho[s] Foster y[e] Sloop Mary from Bahemies
No Passengers.
Sam[ll] Saunders y[e] Sloop Eliz[a] & Mary from Newfoundland
No Passengers.
Joseph Warren y[e] ship Winter-Bourn from Bristoll
Ann Atwood & Child
Mary Battell & Six Servants
3 David Gentleman y[e] Pink, Eliza from Madera
Richard & Patrick French Merchts
John Richardson Gent[m]
Mary ———
Tho[s] Pickendon y[e] ship America from Lisborn
No Passengers.
Sam[ll] Skeel y[e] ship John & Tho[s] from New Castle
Robert Young George Palmer
W[m] Brown John Graham
Ross Ory

July 5 W^m^ Partridge y^e^ ship Eliz^a^ from Surenam
W^m^ Blanchard a Bay Man
6 Timothy Mulford y^e^ Sloop Success from Connecticut
No Passengers.
Phillip Bass y^e^ Sloop Mary from Cape Fransway
No Passengers.
7 Sam^ll^ Pell the Sloop Abigail from Barbados
No Passengers.
Silvanus Hussey y^e^ Sloop Eagle from North Carolina
Humphry Wady a Glover
Edw^d^ Nuby a Cooper
Simon Slocomb y^e^ Sloop Success from Maryland
No Passengers
John Wells the Sloop Experience from Exuena
No Passengers.
9 John Lane y^e^ Sloop Friends Adventure from New Hamshire
No Passengers.
Richard Pitcher y^e^ Snow W^m^ & James from Barbados
No Passengers.
10 Sam^l^ Foye y^e^ Ship Crown Gally from Isle of May
No Passengers.
John Margeson y^e^ Sloop Mercury from New York
Peter Colewell a Cape Maker
11 Benj^a^ Evans y^e^ Sloop Betty from Barbado^s^
Charles Penny a Mercht & his boy
John Higinbothem a Planter.
12 John Aram y^e^ Ship Jollif Gally from London
W^m^ Baker, Marr^n^
Capt Armitage Ditto & His Boy
Francis Dewing Engraver
W^m^ Foster School Master
Jnŏ Richards Johny Tyley M^r^ Wadsworth Marriners
James Painter Abra^m^ Lyon serv^ts^
Eliza Winfield Ditto
Eliza Stewart.
Tho^s^ Lithered y^e^ Ship Mary from London
Capt. Rich^d^ Foster
Capt. Peter Blackstone
M^r^ Robert Butler } Merch^ts^
M^r^ Tho^s^ Phillips }
Capt Calvad a French Marriner.
Joseph Kidder y^e^ Brig^t^ Mich^l^ & Eliză from Barbados
No Passengers.
James Lugmore y^e^ Ship Katherine & Eliz^a^ from Barbados
No Passengers.
14 Joseph Johnson y^e^ Sloop Goodwin from Rhode Island
No Passengers
16 W^m^ Hackleton y^e^ Sloop Boneto from Compeachy
No Passengers
Edward Lucey y^e^ Ship Mary from Jarsy & Falmoth
charles de Curterett Amis Renouf

July Edw[d] Renouf Francis Durel
Phillip Blackmore Francis De Rue
Math[w] Fall Phillip Leblam
& 7 Boys and 2 Girls Servants.
17 Gershom Cobb y[e] sloop Society from Connecticut
Nath[ll] Barbor. Merch[t].
James Goold y[e] Sloop Hopewell from Philadephia
Benj[a] Street. W[m] Person Mar[n]
Benj[a] Holmes. Hannah Cook Spinster
Tho[s] Thomason y[e] Sloop Succeedwell fr[m] North Carolina
No passengers but Mariners
Henry Aurthur y[e] Ship Happy Return from Isle of May
Francis Masters W[m] Stone
Antho[n] Harbourt
18 Tho[s] Porter y[e] Sloop Diamond from Antigua
No Passengers
John Janverin y[e] Ship King George from Surrenam
Phillip Reason Nich[s] Artue Marr[r]
Richard Sprague a Cooper
Rich[d] Chisman y[e] Ship Anna from London
Abra[m] Souter Mech[n] Jn[o] Jackson a Joyner
23 Edward Dennett y[e] Ship Loyal George from London
Martin a Sail Maker
Andrews a Cabbinet Maker
24 Peter Moredock y[e] Sloop Katharine from Long Island
No Passengers
Joseph Allen y[e] Sloop Neptune from New London
No Passengers
W[m] Goold y[e] Sloop Neptune from Annopilas
W[m] Sheriff
Deliverence Blin y[e] Sloop Two Brothers from New London
John Bennett Cordwainer.
25 Phillip Barger y[e] Ship Hannavour Street from Barbados
No Passengers
26 Jeremiah Wilson y[e] Sloop Ann from New York
Benj[a] Smith Chair Maker
27 John Fuller y[e] Brigg[tt] John & Eliza from Barbados
No Passengers
30 Josiah Prince y[e] Sloop Mayflower from Connecticutt
No Passengers
John Jones y[e] Sloop Adventure from South Carolina
No Passengers
John Mitchell y[e] Sloop Hannah & Mary from North Carolina
No Passengers
Tho[s] Smith y[e] Sloop Adventure from Madera
Tho[s] Wright a Marriner
31 Edw[d] Freeman y[e] Sloop Farmers Tryal from North Carolina
No passengers

Sept. Vessels Entred in the Month of September 1716

Allexander Baker $y^e$ Brigg$^t$. Phillip & Mary from Mountseratt
No Passengers
David Arnold $y^e$ Sloop Charles $fr^m$ Annopolis
No Passengers.
3 James Cahoone $y^e$ Sloop Mary $fr^m$ Rhode Island
No Passengers.
Timothy Williamson $y^e$ Sloop Martha $fr^m$. Connecticut
Sarah Strong, Spinster
Robert Holleday
Joseph Bosworth $y^e$ Ship Neptune from Barbados
$W^m$ Brown $Merch^t$
4 Henry Lowder $y^e$ Brigg$^t$. Dilligent $fro^m$ Antigua
Sam$^l$. Royall Merch$^t$. & Bro$^t$.
Frewin a Tallow Chandler.
5 Jeffry Bedgood $y^e$ Ship Eliz$^a$. $fro^m$ S$_t$. Christophers
No Passengers ——
8 Dan$^l$. Jackson $y^e$ Sloop Mayflower $fr^m$. Newheaven
Sarah Cotton Spinster
John Lastly $y^e$ Sloop Speadwell $fr^m$. Jamaica
No Passengers.
10 Jacob Boardman $y^e$ Sloop Eliz$^a$. $fr^m$ N. Carolina
No Passengers
Will$^m$. Walter the Sloop Mayflower $fr^m$. Anopolis
W$^m$. Tipen [?] A Solder
Rich$^d$. Collier $y^e$ Brigg$^t$. Dan$^l$. $fr^m$. Surrenam
Phillip Lewis Marin$^r$.
Miles Rainsbothem $y^e$ Sloop Jane & Mary $fr^m$. No. Carolina
Ebenez$^r$. Allen
11 John Thorp Brigg$^{tt}$: Eliz$^a$. $fr^m$. Lisbon
No Passengers.
John Bonner $y^e$ Sloop Christopher $fr^m$. Barbados
No Passengers
Ebenezer Graves $y^e$ Ship John & William $fr^m$. Compeachy
John Lane Jos. Rogers, Jn$^o$. Woodman Cornelius Mackneroll } Lagunas
William Jarmann $y^e$ Snow Henry $fr^m$. Bristol
W$^m$. Bryan a Marin$^r$.
John Lennard $y^e$ Ship three Maryes $fr^m$. Barbados
No Passengers
14 Henry Richards $y^e$ Pink Rebecca $fr^m$. Topsam
W$^m$. Joanes W$^m$. Pallamer Benj$^a$. Brook Jacob Barnes } Servt$^s$.
18 David Prince $y^e$ Sloop James & Mary $fr^m$. N.Carolina
Jon$^a$ Phelps plant$^{rs}$.
Charles Bull Cabinet Maker
Ebenezer Chamberlain $y^e$. Sloop Martha $fr^m$. N. Carolina
Sam$^l$. Northy a Mariner

Sept. 20 Sam. Roberts y[e] Sloop Eliz[a]. fr[m]. Newfoundland
John Poor & Wife
Jn[o]. Pop Peter Dimond James Comins
Rich[d]. Moncoy Rich[d]. Clark Tho[s]. Warrin
James Semons Tho[s]. Ebdon Amos Velicot
Jn[o]. Chaple Jn[o]. Lecan Robert Webber } Marriners
Antho[y]. Torel Sam[l]. Adams Robert Brooks
Jn[o]. Knot Jn[o]. Arly Jn[o]. Shopin
Jn[o]. Radford Jn[o]. Edwards
George Pumiss y[e] Brigg[t] Joseph & Sarah fr[m]. London & Tenareaf
James Sterling a Merch[t]. & Six of his Marin[s].
Gresham Cobb the Sloop Brothers Society fr[m]. Connecticut
John Hayden
21 Edward Sturgis y[e] Sloop Prosperity from Connecticut
Jn[o]. Darling
David Sturgis Peter King } Farmers
John Abbott y[e] Sloop Seaflower fr[m]. New Hamshire
One Woman & 2 Children
Robert Mires y[e] Brigg[t]. Lamb fr[m]. Compeachy
Josiah Robert a bayman
Jerm[a]. Cogswell a Doctor
24 John Larment y[e] Sloop Adventure fr[m]. Newfoundland
Mark Dem, Pirce Dwyre, Pirce Gent
James Garwarn, Nich[s] Robert, W[m] Warrin
Tho[s] Chevalier, Jn[o]. Chevalier, Jacob Am
John Lebrok, Phillip Lemarmett, Simon Levil
Peirce Leprevet, James Rabay, Tho[s]. Boami } Mariners
Mich[l]. Rabay, Tho[s]. Blondell, Glande Lesage
Bertrem Denisod, Barnard Uherenne, Mich[a]. Thomas
Jn[o] Lovlel, Jearge Parker, John Lecras
Tho[s] Steeme, Thos. Baily Honori Silvester
Ebenezer Fisher y[e] Sloop Katherine fr[m]. St. Thomases
No Passengers
Arnold Gillum y[e] Sloop 4 Friends fr[m]. Connecticut
No Passengers
Peter Murdock y[e] Sloop Katherine fr[m]. Long Island
No Passengers
Dan[l] Frizell y[e] Brigg[t]. Betty fr[m]. Antigua
No Passengers
Willoby Hall y[e] Ship Fortune from New Castle
No Passengers
Isaac Bird y[e] George & Mary fr[m]. Weymoth
W[m]. Gilbert a Merch[t].
John Gale y[e] Barque Carpenter fr[m]. White Heaven
No Passengers
Deliverance Blinn y[e] Sloop 2 Brothers fr[m]. Connecticut
No Passengers
Tho[s]. Jenkins y[e] Brigg[t]. Success fr[m]. Bilboa & Cows
No Passengers

Sept. 24 Thos. Daggett $y^e$ Ship Esther $fr^m$. London
Rich$^d$. Quick, Rich$^d$ Mohaer }
Jn$^o$. Pressin wife & Child } Marin$^s$
Jane Rogers & 3 Children }
Thomas Potts $y^e$ Ship Anna & Mary $fr^m$. Bristoll
Tho$^s$. Carslake a Merch$^t$
Tho$^s$. Barnat Jn$^o$. Moffat Rich$^d$. Revess & Wife Marin$^s$.
Thos. Goodfellow a husbandman
Jacob Spikman a Cooper
Giles Lester Clark
Joseph New Shipwright Thos. Gilbert & Serv.
Tho$^s$. Dimond the Ship Dove $fr^m$. London
John Frizel a Lad
Patrick Gaskin a Gent$^l$.
Tho$^s$. Goodale Merch$^t$.
William Beckman $y^e$ Sloop Speadwell $fr^m$. New York
Mr. —— Peck a Leather Dresser

25 Tho$^s$. Fleming $y^e$ Sloop Grahound $fr^m$. South Carolina
Jn$^o$. Ranchen Merch$^t$ & his Wife
Jn$^o$. Markland Doc$^r$.
Dan$^l$. Dean Plant$^r$.
Jn$^o$. Demick Edw$^d$. Demerick }
Jn$^o$. Hipingstall Jn$^o$. Pollock } Mariners
Will$^m$. Hipingstall }
Sam$^l$. Cutler Sailmaker
Jon$^a$. Sharp $y^e$ Ship Marblehead $fr^m$. Holland
Jacob Wendall a Merch$^t$.

27 Richard Thomas $y^e$ Ship Thomas from Jamaica
No Passengers

29 George Marshall $y^e$ Brigg$^t$ Mary $fr^m$. Barbados
No Passengers.

Dated primo October 1716
Dan. Russell, Comm.

Imported from Hallyfax in the Scoon$^r$ Patience W$^m$ Phipps

Passengers Names

| | | |
|---|---|---|
| Patrick Power | John Ryan, | Rich$^d$. Power |
| David Dunn | Edmond Magrath | Thom$^s$. Power |
| Patrick Phealan | John Cuff, | James Cosquer |
| Micheal Nevil | Thomas Glody, | Thomas Fitzgearld |
| Phillip Ryan | Hugh Keen | |

The above are Fishermen

Aug 19. 1762. W$^m$ Phipps

The List of the Passengers on Board the Brigg Elizabeth.
Gentlemen in the Cabin.

| | |
|---|---|
| Mr Lewis Mercht. | Capt. Sheppard, Marriner. |
| Mr Thomas " | Capt Cooke Landed at Nova Scotia. |
| Capt. Willm Sheppard, Marriner. | Mr Gill " " " " |
| Mr Williams, Mercht | Mr Shaahay " " " " |
| Capt Hosier, Marriner. | Capt. Johnson, Marriner |

The Shipes Company in the Sturage

| | | |
|---|---|---|
| Gilbert Northey—mate, | Wm Frygall, | Saml. Breed, |
| John Sealy, | James orchard, | Thomas Hamilton, |
| John Casey, | Wm. Shannan, | Ed. Shaahay, |
| Amos Boorn, | Thomas Hoodley, | Abraham Haldridge, |
| Christopher Frances, | John Darge, | Jacob Luke. |
| Wm Edgiscoate | | |

The Famleys

Henrey Bradford Ship carpenter one Wife sister and 4 children
Wm Pulling, Mason and his wife
Wm Hyman Fisherman and 2 woman and 4 children
Joseph Pottle ship carpenter one woman and 6 "
Philip Marshal, Fisherman one woman 2 "
Ed. Freeman, Fisherman 3 "
Mathew Greenslet " one woman 3 "
Joseph Newel " one woman 1 "
George Wood Taylor one woman 2 "
James Daw one woman 3 " Landed at Nova Scotia — Frs Hearn
Emanuel Stow, Fisherman two women 5 children
John Waldon carpenter one woman 1 child.

I. Office Boston Aug 24. 1762.

A list of Pasingers Brought oup from Halifax In the Sloop Swaller Samuel Doggett, Mastar

| | | |
|---|---|---|
| Doct. McComb | Royal Regiment | Halifax |
| Neail his Sarvent | | ditto |
| Mr —— Sanders | marchant | Mariland |
| William Philips | Sandwich — | Trader |
| William Huston? | Boston — | Printer |
| Petar Aiers, | Manchestor | Fisherman |
| Mosses Lowel, | Rowley | Trader |
| Jesiah Molten, | Wannam | Salar |
| Samuel Palmer | Rowly | Trader |
| Seth Blossam, | Barnstabl | Trader |
| John Poor | Iarland | Book keeper |
| Elihu Wordrof } Thomas Peach } | New York | |

Mason & Wife and five Children Molbary

John Dobl } Job Baxter } Boston

I. Office Boston May 17. 1762

## PORT ARRIVALS — IMMIGRANTS.

[The first name is evidently that of the captain of the vessel.]

### 1763.

Mar 16 Hugh Hunter, Ship Devonshire from London
Capt. Sam. Dashwood. Capt. Willm Scott, Marriners.
Mr John Lewis. Mr John Hatton, Merchants
18 Marlaugh McCarrell, Sloop Phenix from Louisburgh
Lieut Barnes of the 45th Regiment. His Wife & 2 Servts
22 Seth Chipman Sloop Abigl from North Carolina
Phelix Dunn a Marinr
25 Joseph Ingraham Schoonr Speedwell from St Martins
Capt. Robt Follett Marrinr
28 Thoms Valentine Brigc Vanson N. York.
Mrs Houldies wife to Mr Houldies of New York.
Lydia Wisell a Mollato

April 2 Hugh Orr Schoonr Betsey from Maryland
John Lablanch } Simon White } Frenchmen that went from this Province
Nathl Atwood Sloop Betsey from Hallifax
John Bels, Mercht. Peter Yengle Traider
Patrick Poor, Taylor
Joseph Williston, Andw Master, John Roach, Luke Herwell, Frans Mores, Adam Inster } Farmers.
Joseph Elisken, Willm Pake, Saml Bryon, Edwd Hier. } Sailors
Enoch Creken — Soldier.
4 Thoms Frazier Sloop Phenix N. Carolina
Morris Dunlay } John ——— } Marrinrs
5 Bellingham Watts Schoonr Charmg Salley [from] Providence
Mr David Love a Trader
Capt Abrahm Gubuatt Marrinr.
9 Crowell Hatch Sloop Salley from N. Carolina
Mr Read a Planter
Capt Gilbert Ash Marrinr
15 Saml Gorham Sloop Baltimore from Philadelphia
Mr Cumings Mercht
18 Nathl Shiverick Sloop Lovey from Philadelphia.
Capt. Everson of Salem Marrinr & His Mate.
20 Calvin Deleno Sloop Dove from N. Carolina
Mrs Moor a Widow
Mr Archabd Gallaspe Mercht
21 George Bartlet Sloop Speedwell from Maryland
Miss's Jane & Peggy Gorden for Hallifax
" Jonth Snow Sloop Scorton Polley from Philedelpha
Mr John Johnson Mercht.
25 James Dickey Sloop Lucy from Hallifax
Jams Dennis a Soldier & His wife.

Susanna Farr wife to a Soldier
John Forguson a Trader
Mr Yearley a Mercht
Jams Sherman a Jewiler
Elizth Richards a Spinster
Mrs Green belonging to Hallifax.
27 Willm Jernigan Sloop Brittania from Maryland
Wm King a Marrinr
Josiah Gorham Sloop Iiana from Philidelpha
Mr. Wm. Black Mercht.
May 3 Edmd Morton. scoonr Dove from Hallifax
Mrs Gerrish Wife to Benja Gerrish Esqr
Mrs Gray wife to Mr Gray
Messrs Jacob & John Wendell Mercht
Capt Small & two sailors
Capt Black " four sailors.
9 Thoms Goodspeed Sloop Desire from Connecticutt
David Rowland Esqr & Daughter.
10 Elnathan Jones Scooner Susanh from Granada.
Capt Lawson, Capt Mumford & Boy, Mr Giles & two Boys. } Marriners
Nathl Tompson Sloop Defiance from Philadelpa
Mr Morrison, Mr Combs, Mr Smithers, Marriners
John McKean Scoonr Lark from Havanah
Mr Atkins a Mercht
11 Thomas Jones Sloop Tryal from N. Carolina
Mr Thoms Shaw, Mr Jno Conney, Mr Mick } Traders.
Peter Newman Marrinr
Mrs Mary Pitman & her Brother Children to Mr Pitman, Hatter.
14 Nathl Doan Sloop Polly from Connecticut
Mrs Starr Wife to Cap Starr, & his son
Elizth Snow Spinster
Joana Green Daughter to Mr Green Brasier & three men belonging to Connecticut
Robt Calef ship Volunteer from London
Cap Elliot, Thos How, Hugh McCoy, Wm Renolds } Marriners.
21 Nathl Williams Snow Priscilla from St Tubes [Saint Ubes]
Mr Thoms Cassey Mercht
— Zachh Gage schooner Tryal from Martinico
Capt Job Bradford Marriner
Doct. Loring
4 Marriners
23 Mark Fernald sloop Friends Adventure from Piscataqua
Ebenr Hodskins, Jonthn Wetam, Geden Watam, Jacob Bridgham } Soldiers

23 Sam[l] Windson Sloop Unity from Annapolis
Mr Reed a Farmer
Mr Fletcher a Ditto
Mr Barnes a Ditto.
30 Jam[s] Dean Sloop Defiance from Hallifax.
List not given in.
June 4 Joseph Chapman Sloop Ranger from Connecticut
Mary Edwards Spinster.
9 Jam[s] Dickey Sloop Lucy from Fort Cumberland
Mr Charles Chalton a Farmer
13 Caleb Symmes Brig[t] Catherine from Guaodilope
Henry Vassel Esq & 3 children to His care.
17 W[m] Wimble Sloop Stanford from New York
8 House Carpenters belonging to this town.
" Ephraim Dean Schoon[r] Murrey from New F[d] Land
Cap[n] Bulley a Marrin[r]
Mr Button } Merch[ts]
Mr Brock }
20 Epes Greenough Sloop 3 Friends from Piscatuqua
Miss Eliz[th] Bryan Spinster
M[rs] Han[h] Day wife to a Merch[t]
— Nath[l]. Shiverick Sloop Lovey from Philadelphia
David Scott, Weaver
Mr Boyes Brazier
M[rs] Catherine Horrick wife to a Marriner
Frank a Marriner
21 John Pinder Sloop Salley from N. Carolina
John Atkins Trader
— Hen[y] Haughton Schoon[r] Betsey from N. Carolina
Mr W[m] Thompson Merch[t]
22 Tho[s] Mitchel Schoon[r] Glasgow from N. F[d] Land
Mr Hamilton a Lieut[t]
M[rs] Warren Wife to a Soldier & 2 Children
27 Step[n] Bourroughs Schoon[r] Mercury from Connect
M[rs] Clark of Connecticut
M[rs] Han[h] & Esther Shelton of Ditto
M[rs] Abig[l] Lewis Ditto
" David Codner Schoon[r] Polley from New F. Land
Cap[n] Sam[l] Row, Cap[n] Swetland }
Cap[n] Jonas Bass, Cap[n] Tead } Marriners
Cap[n] Hall, }
James Orr Snow Jenney from Glasgow
13 Sailors
Will[m] Smith a Lockmaker. Alex[r] Willson a Brewer
Will[m] Barcly a Smith. Mr Rob[t] Shelork Merch[t]
Epes Greenough Sloop three Friends from Piscatuqua
Mary Prout, Deborah Prout & Abig[l] Lang Spinsters
George Hastam Sloop Yarmoth from Hallifax
Cap[n] Keen, Cap[n] Will[m] Barron. }
Lieut Abrah[m] Tuckerman. } Provential
Lieut Nathan Deleno. } Officers
Lieut Isaac Tuckerman }

Lieut Michael Martin } Provential
Doc[t] Moor } Officers
5 Sergeants Ditto
30 Privats Ditto Soldiers
10 Women Viz[t]. 14 children Viz[t]

| | |
|---|---|
| Mary Tuckerman | Eliz[th] Keen |
| Ann Evens | Jane Warner |
| Mary Ryan | Char[s] Warner |
| Marg[t] McKimm | Marg[t] Warner |
| Mary Grey | Mary Tuckerman |
| Lydia Keen | Bartho Tuckerman |
| Hannah Morse | Marg[t] Akins |
| Mary Gault | Ann Gault |
| Margert Akins | Lydia Keen |
| Jane Warner | Abig[l] Keen |
| | Joanna Keen |
| | Rob[t] Keen |
| | Lydia Ryan |
| | Ann Evans |

} 42 men
10 women
14 children

Isaac Phillips Schoon[r] Nancy from Cape Breton
John Monlony, Cap[t] Curr. Mich[l] Colman } Merch[ts]
John Bowles, M[r] Shepard. Edw[d] Terrel }
Jam[s] Carrol, Taylor John Dillon, Marrin[r]
Doct Rogers, Catharine Ceasey
Will[m] Morton Brig[t] Industry from Georga
M[r] David Conzenham Planter
And[w] Gardner Brig[t] New Swallow from New York.
Passengers not given in
W[m] Homer Schoon[r] Ranger from Fyall
M[r] Char[s] Milton.
Epes Greenough Sloop three Friends from Piscatuqua
Cap[n] Sam[l] Darling }
Rich[d] Marshall } Marrin[r]
Will[m] Thomas }
M[rs]. Mary Sherburn & Her son belongs to Piscatuqua.

July 25 John Dean Brig[t] True Britton from Jamaica
M[r] Nathan Butler a Gentleman

27 Benj[n] Stedman Schoon[r] Humbird from Jamaica
Mr Will[m] Perrey } Merch[t]
Mr Jam[s] White }

28 Jon[th] Clarke Sloop Sherburn from Cape Sables
Jon[th] Worth Farmer
Elisha Coffen Fisherman
M[rs] Doan wife to a Farmer.

30 Jos[h] Dobel Schoon[r] Nancy from N. F. Land
Cap[t] John Pele Marrin[r]

Aug. 2 Helier Thoumy Brig[t] Royal Charlotte from the Havanah.
Lawrance Memy a Boy that was cast a Way.

8 And[w] Newell Schoon[r] Ann from St Eustatia
Lieut Phillips & His Serv[t]
Cap[n] Walker Marr[r]

12 Fran$^{s}$ Wells Brig$^{t}$ Hannah from Martineco
Mr Will$^{m}$ Ramsey Merch$^{t}$
13 Eph$^{rm}$ M$^{c}$Farland Sloop Peggy from N. F. Land.
M$^{r}$ Bosweth a Merch$^{t}$.
Hugh M$^{c}$Phillimy Sloop Unity from Hallifax
Josiah Nuttage
Will$^{m}$ Wheat } Traders.
John Griffin
John Peck House Carpenter.
15 Corn$^{s}$ Crocker jun$^{r}$ Schoon$^{r}$ Lucretia from N. Carolina
Cap$^{n}$ Allen.
Nath$^{l}$ Doan Sloop Polley from Connecticut
M$^{rs}$ Melone a Widow
M$^{r}$ Wells, M$^{r}$ John Norton Farmers.
Jam$^{s}$ Peirepoint Sailor
18 Nath$^{l}$ Shiverick Sloop Lovey from Philadelphia
Cap$^{n}$. Gabrel Leblon
Doct. Torrey [?] & His Wife
W$^{m}$ Brown a Painter
Jonath Herd a Taylor
Miss Nancy Macksford to the care of M$^{r}$ Maxwell.
20 Jam$^{s}$ Dickey Sloop Lucy from Fort Cumberland
David Hopkins a Farmer
Will$^{m}$ Sharp a Seaman
Jane Danford wife to a Soldier at Fort Cumberland.
25 Nath. Atwood Sloop Sally from Louisbourgh
Sam$^{l}$ Bonner Merch$^{t}$
John Coverly, Clerk to the Hospital at Hallyfax
Joseph Peirce a Carpenter
26 Noah Doggett Scoon$^{r}$ Abigail from Bristoll
James Russell Merch$^{t}$
Cap Duff
Jn$^{o}$ English } Marriners.
29 W$^{m}$ Wimble Sloop Stamford from N. York
M$^{rs}$ Cowdry & three children, wife to M$^{r}$ Cowdry a Clerk
Sept 2 Benj$^{a}$ Homer Sloop Swallow from Quebec
M$^{r}$ Will$^{m}$ Dooley
M$^{r}$ David Orrick } Marrin$^{r}$
27 Soldiers
5 Ephraim Dean Schoon$^{r}$ Murray from N. F. Land
Soldiers.
13 John Waterman Sloop Deborah [from] Philadelphia
Cap$^{t}$ Lamb
M$^{r}$ White a Soap Boyler.
14 Revell Munroe Sloop Advice from N. Carolina
M$^{r}$ Parker Quince a Merch$^{t}$
Roger Moor a Youth for Education.
24 Joshua Beal Schoon$^{r}$ Desire from Hallifax
The Rev$^{d}$ Mess$^{rs}$ Manning & Sutton
M$^{r}$ Daniel Sigorney Mercht

Hen[y] Clarey
M[r] John Wakefield
Step[n] Walker
Norman M[c]Cloud
W[m] Dougharty
Joseph Collick
Daniel Kenney — Soldiers
W[m] Wood
W[m] M[c]Garth
Sam[ll] Killpatrick
Alex Brown
W[m] Campbell
Peter Lebauch

Roger Ryan a Soldier & his wife
Sam[l] Stebbens Scoon Eliz from Quebeck
Cap Roger Bartlet & his men
Cap. Habersham — Marriners

26 Linsford Morey Scooner Speedwell from Bristoll
John Harris
Thom[s] Cain — Marriners
W[m] Screech

Andr[w] Jackson a Distiller

29 James Dickey Sloop Lucy from Cumberland
Cap[t] John Walker
M[r] Robert Wadley a Brewer
M[r] Jn[o] Edy
M[r] King — Farmers
M[r] Gardner

Oct. 5 Lott Hall Sloop Endeavour from Quebec
M[r] Charles Jerham a Merch[t].

10 Hugh M[c] Phillimy Sloop Unity from Halifax
M[r] Walker, Tim[o] Dawey, Tho[s] Hubbard
David M[c]Lane, Desire Haws. — Soldiers.
Tho[s] Paul Carpenter
Barber Walker Traider.
Phillis Henry Wife to a Painter at Halifax
Tho[s] Simmons Sailor
Ellery Bridge Wife to a Surveyor at Luningburg
Jam[s] Freeman a Lad for Education

Jon[n] Mansfield Sloop Dove from Connect[t].
M[rs] Rebecca Russell a Widow

Eleaz Hathaway Sloop Ranger from New F[d] Land
James Morton
Eben[r] Avery — Sailors.

Rob[t] Farthing Ship Adm[l] Boscowen from N. Castle
M[r] Lowdey a Cooper.

13 John Philips Brig[t] Industry from St Eustatia
M[rs] Hawks & Son

Fran[s] Chase Sloop Baltimore from Philad[a]
Jam[s] Renolds Merch[t]
M[r] Dean.

17 Chars.? Andrews Sloop Mary from Connect$^{t}$.
M$^{r}$ John Brown & 2 Boys & 1 Girl to His care
18 John Tyler Brig$^{t}$ Kitty from S$^{t}$ Martins
M$^{r}$ Isaac Waterman a Merch$^{t}$.
18 Josiah Loring Brig$^{t}$ Peace & Plenty from London
Cap$^{n}$ Tho$^{s}$ Tatham, Cap$^{n}$ Robert Young Marriners
M$^{r}$ Jonath$^{n}$ Amory, M$^{r}$ Will$^{m}$ Greenleaf Merch$^{ts}$
Doc$^{t}$ Jn$^{o}$ Greenleaf
John — ? Clark a Youth to the Care of M$^{r}$ Head
Jam$^{s}$ Smellidge Carpenter
Jn$^{o}$ Bell, Jam$^{s}$ Boyard, Joseph Phillips, Jn$^{o}$ Bound M$^{r}$ Ellis } Marrin$^{rs}$
20 Justus Taylor Sloop Three Partners from Connect$^{t}$
M$^{rs}$ Wendell a Widow
M$^{rs}$ Hannah Doan Spinster
Sam$^{l}$ Soul Sloop Abig$^{l}$ from N. Carolina
Rob$^{t}$ Jordan a Lad to the Care of the Captain
21 Will$^{m}$ Hayes Brig$^{t}$ Wolf from Kirkwell
Tho$^{s}$ Trail a Lad to the Care of Jam$^{s}$ Trail of this Town.
28 Barns Coffen Schoon$^{r}$ Dolphen from N. F$^{d}$. Land
Tho$^{s}$ Darbey, Edw$^{d}$ Morrosey, Mich$^{l}$ Coleman Arch$^{d}$ Lake, Jam$^{s}$ Fitzpatrick, Abel Smith, W$^{m}$ Haven. } Mar-rin$^{rs}$.
Jam$^{s}$ Montgomerie Ship Doglass from Scotland.
Lynall Cambal, Symon Corled, Mich$^{l}$ M$^{c}$Carney, Ralph O Donal. W$^{m}$ Harreson, W$^{m}$ Creer, Rob$^{t}$ Corled, Jn$^{o}$ Gulles, W$^{m}$ Seal, Jn$^{o}$ Creer, Jn$^{o}$ Doughny, W$^{m}$ Morrison, Marg$^{t}$ Quark, Eliz$^{th}$ Christian, Ann Moore, Margret Callo, Eliz$^{th}$ Tear, Jane Kelly, Jane Nean, Cather$^{e}$ Corkan, Eliz$^{th}$ Carran.
M$^{r}$ Moor a Cooper, M$^{r}$ Harrison Gentlem$^{n}$
Cap$^{t}$ Christian. Marrin$^{r}$ W$^{m}$ Kelley, Shoemaker.
31 Peter Doyle Sloop two Sisters from N. F$^{d}$ Land.
Cap$^{n}$ Cook, Cap$^{n}$ Ceasey Marrn$^{rs}$
George Swan
—— Baker
Rich$^{d}$ Carpenter
Will$^{m}$ Copper
John Cooper
W$^{m}$ Cooper
Elias Halstaf
Rober$^{t}$ Feature
John Pills
Geo Glover
W$^{m}$ Bishop
Fran$^{s}$ Murphey
Patrick White
Patrick Dumphey
Peter Provo
John Patch
Will$^{m}$ Bradley.

Nov 3 John Tozer Brig[t] Swift from New Castle
John Carr Sailor
—— Gilroy Do.
7 Valentine Baker Snow Bristol from New F[d] Land
Rich[d] Waterman Merch[t]
Eph[m] Dean Schoon[r] Molley from Hallifax
Lieut[s] Newton & Weston officers
M[r] Greenleaf Doct[s]. Cap[n] Scott Marrin[s] and sundry others as per List now sent.
Abel Badger Sloop Success from Philed[a]
List not yit givin in.
7 Josiah Beal Schoon[r] Desire from Hallifax
not given in
9 John Blake ship Adventure from London
List not given in.
15 Rob[t] M[c]Curdy Sloop Endeavour from Hallifax
Passengers as p[r] List
Andrew Simonton sloop Seaflower from Quebec
M[r] Burnet an Ensign
M[r] M[c]Ferson a Serg[t]
M[r] M[c]Ferson a Corporel and Wife
M[r] Gridley of this Town.
Char[s] Robison Ship Diligence from Glasgow
Rob[t] Stevenson, Merch[t]. And[w] Turner D[o] W[m] Burten D[o]
Hugh Smille, David Peters, And[w] Anderson
Rob[t] Steil, Jn[o] Banantin Mariners
Jam[s] Pillogrove, Quantine Leach, W[m] Fullerton
Jn[o] Shannon, John Miller, W[m] Linkletre } Sailors
John M[c]Intire, Rob[t] Orr, Jn[o] Jack, Rob[t] Moor
Hugh Moody, Taylor
Amos Hatch Sloop Industry from New F[d] Land
Passengers as p[r] List
Adam Hall Sloop Ranger from Hallifax
List not given in.
21 Thom Simonton Sloop Susan[a] from Louisburgh
Benj[a] Allen a Discharged Soldier
Matthead Eareckson Sloop Semerset from Maryland
Oliver White a Carpen[t] M[rs] Fran[s] Holzand Wife to a Sailor and Lad to the Care of Ditto.
24 Josiah Knowles Sloop Nancy from N. Carolina
M[r] Will[m] Ahajar Merch[t]
25 Will[m] Wimble Sloop Stanford from N. York.
M[r] Jones a Serg[t] & His Wife.
Step[n] Hayter Sloop Phenix from Margalett
Timothy Kelham a Fisherman his Wife & Servant.
Dec[r] Thomas Austin Sloop Peggy from N. Found Land.
Partrick Droham Tho[s] Glody
Simon Hannahan And[r] Simoning,
Rich[d] Welsh, Jn[o] Tobing, Jn[o] Shepard, } Sailors and Fishermen
Phillip Stapltou, Jam[s] Roach, W[m] Mady
Ja[s] Forley, Jn[o] Delaney, Christ[r] Collings.

| | | |
|---|---|---|
| Jn$^{o}$ Poor. W$^{m}$ Potter | Mich$^{ll}$ Ash | Sailors and Fishermen |
| Nich$^{ls}$ Buttler. | Jn$^{o}$ D$^{e}$ Loyd. | |
| Tho$^{s}$ Buttler. | Richard Surrey | |
| Barth$^{ll}$ Mansfield | Edw$^{d}$ Poor | |
| Selvester Poor | Mich$^{ll}$ Fling | |
| Partrick Felleter | W$^{m}$ Keeting | |
| Jn$^{o}$ Drece | Mich$^{ll}$ Keeting | |
| Sam$^{l}$ Dower | Barn$^{i}$ Green | |
| Rich$^{d}$ Fleming | Christ$^{h}$ Barret | |
| Partrick Power | Tho$^{s}$ Murphey | |
| Partrick Shallow | W$^{m}$ She | |
| Jn$^{o}$ Gosswell | Partick Killey | |
| Henry Gosswell | Jam$^{s}$ Kennedy | |
| Jam$^{s}$ Nowling. | W$^{m}$ Murphey. | |

James Stewart an Engineer and his Son William.

Nath$^{l}$ Atwood Sloop Swallow from Hallyfax
Passenger List not given in
Cap$^{n}$ Nath$^{l}$ Atwoods Passengers.
Nath$^{l}$ Whitmarsh Carpenter
Israel Loring Do
Joshua Nutting
Joshua Coll Farmer
John Poor
— Marcy Reier
Geo Carr sailor
Rob$^{t}$ Wither
Josiah Hamon
Thom$^{s}$ Wincams
M$^{rs}$ Marcy Maglene How & Serv$^{t}$

19 Thomas Dixey Brig$^{e}$ Pell pack$^{t}$ from London
Cap$^{n}$ Hulme, Cap$^{n}$ Obear, Cap$^{n}$ Mawdley. } Marrin$^{rs}$
John Shores, Leon$^{d}$ Lewis, Jos$^{h}$ Buck, Jos$^{h}$ Pelum, W$^{m}$ Macknutt } Sailors

Rob$^{t}$ Jervis Brig Hannah from London
M$^{r}$ Gray a Barber & His wife
Cap$^{n}$ Tossey, Cap$^{n}$ Stone, Cap$^{n}$ Holmes } Marriners

28 Joshua Benel [?] Schoon$^{r}$ Desire from Hallifax
Cap$^{n}$ Jn$^{o}$ Dier, M$^{r}$ Briant, Joseph Smith } Marrin$^{s}$. John Keeth Traider.

27 Ephraim Dean Sloop Two Brothers from Hallifax
M$^{r}$ ONeal a Trader

30 W$^{m}$ Fogo Sloop Molly from Cumberland
M$^{r}$ Danks a Farmer
Lewis Fitch Gerrald Scoon$^{r}$ Deborah from Quebeck
M$^{r}$ John Austin a Merch$^{t}$

*31 Will^m Fogo Sloop Charm^g Molly from Fort Cumberland
Mr Danks a Farmer [Dup. Entry]

**1764.**

Jan^y. 19 Sam^l Stibbins Schoon^r Eliz^th from Hallifax
Mr Joseph Brightman Merch^t
Mr Camble
N. Chandler
Isaac Sturdavent
W^m Olford
Mr Gillett
Mrs Abig^l Starr a Spinster.
25 Jeram^h Webber Schoon^r Molley from Rh^o Island
Mrs Wilson Wife to a Carpenter
Doctor Gillson
27 Henry Johnson Schoon^r Nelley from Domingo.
Cap^n John Allen } Marrin^rs
Cap^n Conner }
31 Joseph Baley Sloop Betsey from S^t Christophers
Cap^n John Crooker Marrin^r.
Feb 13 Andrew Gardner Brig^t New Swallow from South Carolina
Captain Cowen Marriner
a French Pilot belong to Quebec
14 Nath^l Atwood Sloop Swallow from Hallifax
Josiah Nutwich a Carpenter
17 Hugh Orr Schoon^r Betsey from Hispaniola
Cap^n Dan^l Shaw Cap^n Rich^d Dunn. } Marrin^rs
March 1 Ephraim Dean Sloop two Brothers from Hallifax
Doct Kannady His wife & Serv^t
Mr Grant a Soldier His wife & 3 Children
Gardner Greenleaf a Shoemaker
John Mackdonel a Butcher
John Donlop a Gentlem^n
Willm. Donlop a Cooper
John Demount a Butcher
Paul Padert a Marriner
Rich^d Harris Sloop two Friends from New London
Mr Drue a ship Carpenter
5 Will^m Marshall Brig^t Success from Hallifax
Lieut Fran^s Green of 40 Reg^t
Sam^l Baley Hatter
9 Samuel Snow Sloop Ruby [from] Louisbourgh
John Keith a Soldier
Alex Birchford a Marriner.
19 John Goodwin Sloop Charm^g Nancy from Philadelphia
Mr John Burns a Merch^t.
20 Sam^l Concklin Sloop William from New York
Mr Pease an aprentice to Doc^t Gilson.
John Whealden Marrin^r

21 David Phipps Sloop Industry from North Carolina
Sam[l] Service & Merch[t]
31 Benj[n] Cobb Sloop Eliz[th] from North Carolina
Cap[n] Doan & 4 Sailors
M[r] Williams } Merch[t]
M[r] Dixon }
David Heal Marrin[r]
31 Nath[l] Fellows Schoon[r] two Friends from Cadiz
Cap[n] Philip Bass & 22 Seamen
M[r] And[w] Hall Merch[t]
Apr 2 George Mitchel Sloop Charm[g] Molley from Annapolis
John Winchester
Eben[r] Connet
Gosef Downe
M[rs] Kent Wife to a Farmer & Her Son
M[rs] Fansworthey Wife to a Ditto
Sarah Hiden a Spinster
4 John Doubleday Schoon[r] Industry [from] S[t] Martins
M[r] Brumit Sailor & Wife
Shuball Coffin Schoon[r] Hawke from London
James Merrypine, John Ramshire } Sailors
John Noble James —— }
2 Rob[t] Calef Ship Hale Galley from London
Cap[n] Marshall Marrin[r]
Doct Marshall
M[r] Coats Merch[t]
Cap[n] Edmund Wendell Marrin[r]
4 Thom[s] Mitchel Sloop 2 Sisters [from] Louisburgh
M[rs] Brown & son Wife to a Carpenter of this Town
Benj[a] Bears Schoon[r] thankfull [from] Rh[o] Island
M[r] Leonard a Carpenter.
9 Nath[l] Atwood Sloop Swallow from Hallifax
Thom[s] Wheelen Merch[t]
Joseph Cook Traider
Joseph Cowell Butcher
Mich[l] Ray a Taylor
Gabrel Micher Ditto
Mich[l] Buckelay of Marblehead.
18 Prince Hawes Schoon[r] Providence from N. Carolina
Will[m] Larken Sailor
19 Christ[r] Higgins Sloop Ruby from Connect[t]
M[r] Jn[o] Barrell
M[rs] Sarah Edwards
21 Rhodes Haven Sloop Willingmind [from] N. York
Tho[s] Casney Taylor & His Wife & Serv[t] } for
Char[s] Morry a Ditto His wife & 2 children } cape
Ponly William a Ditto His wife & 3 children } Britton
30 Will[m] Brown Sloop Dolphen from Mountserrat
Nancy Webb a Spinster
May 2 Hugh McPhillimy Sloop Unity from Hallifax
Cap[n] Hamilton in the 45[th] Reg[t] & 2 sons.
5 Sailors

Will^m^ Fisher Schoon^r^ Fishhawk from Virginia
Cap^n^ Elijah Tillman Marrin^r^
5 Nath^l^ Coffin Ship Boston pack^t^ from London
Mr Briggs Holloway, Merch^t^
Cap^n^ Nath^l^ Phillips, Cap^n^ Will^m^ Lad. } Marrin^rs^
Cap^n^ Jam^s^ Parr M^r^ Kentisby }
W^m^ Wallis Sailmaker
7 Howard Jacobson Ship Boscowen from Ditto [London]
M^r^ John Lane } Merch^ts^
M^r^ Sam^l^ Goldthwight }
8 Alex^r^ Inglish Brig^t^ Salley from Providence
M^r^ Bradford Gentle^n^
W^m^ Jones Carpenter
Eph^m^ Tray Ditto
Sam^l^ Hamonway Paint^r^
8 Josiah Knowles Sloop Ranger [from] N. Carolina
Doct. Edw^d^ Morey
Tho^s^ Larken Sailmaker
Elnath^n^ Smith Traider
Lemuel Week Sloop Falmouth from Philadelphia
M^r^ Howard a Merch^t^
W^m^ Chambers Brig^t^ Pembroke from N. Castle
M^r^ Jos^h^ Williams Merch^t^.
14 Theop^s^ Simonton Scoon^r^ Mary from N. York.
Cap^n^ Lovegrove his Wife & 3 children going to Hallyfax
Benj Welch a Sailor.
Rich^d^ Southcot Snow W^m^. & Mary from Bristoll
Cap Rich^d^ Baker & serv^t^.
Hugh Hunter ship Devonshire from London
John Robinson Esq^r^ Collector for R. Island
M^r^ Caleb Blanchard }
M^r^ Edm^d^ Quincy, Tert^s^ } Merchants.
M^r^ Thomas Russell }
Cap^n^ Archibald Denmore } Marriners
M^r^ Turner }
M^r^ Clark belonging to the Paper Manufac^ty^
16 Benj Friswell Sloop Yarmouth from South Carrolina
M^r^ Tho^s^ Conn a Planter & his son.
18 Tho^s^ Vallentine Brig^t^ Vanson from S. Martins.
John Emmes & Nich^s^ Honneyman Marriners
21 Peter Taylor Brig Weymouth from Barbadose
M^r^ Thom^s^ Allen, a Gen^m^ his Two sisters & there Two Children
M^r^ W^m^ Scott a Farmer.
Sam^l^ Pearson ship Sam^l^ & Betsey from New Castle
Margrett a Serv^t^
Peter Taylor Brig^t^ Weymoth from Barbados }
M^r^ Thom^s^ Allen Gentleman, His two sisters & their Children } Dup. ent.
M^r^ Will^m^ Scott a Farmer }
30 W^m^ Cluston Brig^t^ Hound from Ireland.

Capt. Sciler
Wm Coutes, John Carton, Duck Kenned, John Cotter, Corns Obrum, Chars Riney, } Servants
Catherine Odonely, Onne Soloven
Michl Claire, Cooper; Willm Watts, Traider.
Barbery Watts, Spinster. Cathere Riney Spinster

June 1 David Sage Sloop Azuba from Connt.
Amasey Jones Traider

7 Thoms Mathews Sloop Success from Philada
The Revd Mr Rollenbuckler & His Clerke
Mr Harris a Traider.

11 Rhodes Haven Sloop Willingmind from New York
Jacob Derb Shoemaker
Mr Delremple an Officer

12 Benjm Homer Sloop Swallow from Hallifax
Gregory Townshend Esq.
Mrs Phillis Mrs Blagdon Mrs Fairbanks.
Capn Carrel Capn Mc. Thelomy Marrinrs
Josh Carrel Butcher
Mr Jones, Mr Clarke, Mr McNeal Carpenter & a Dutchman

19 Thoms Mitchell Sloop two Sisters [from] Louisburg
Lieut Bowen of ye 45th Regt His wife & child
Capn Hatherman & Servt
Doct Simpson. John Bulling a Frenchman

21 Archibd McFerren Sloop Hannah from Nova Scotia.
Wm Gillmore Jno Kelly James McNutt Wm Logan David Blackmore } Farmers.

23 George Mitchell Sloop Charmg Molley from Annapolis Royall
Daniel Creon, Robt Minga Jno Hendry } Farmers
Mrs Rise Mrs Marshal there Husbands Farmers at Annapolis
James Shannon a Schoolmaster
Mrs Lawley a Widow & her daughter Both going for England.

25 Wm Deverson Ship Mary from London
Revd Mr Hubbard & Mr Jarvis both belonging to Connecticut.
Benja Seward Scoon Little Fortescue from Anquilla
Capn Wm Vernon his Wife and sister

26 Tho Parke Snow Friendship from Madera
Mr John Desousa [?] a Mercht

27 Willm Satchwell Brigt Nancy from N. Fd. Land
John Allward Jeffry Gadridge Jno Crispin Richd Wedden } Marrinrs

27 Richd Newsham Sloop Dolphen [from] Dominico
Mr Warner Mercht

28 John Doubleday Schoon[r] Industry from N. Carolina
Cap[n] Nath Williams
July 2 Abner Stocking Schoon[r] Tryal from Connect[t]
M[rs] Sarah Snow Spinster.
6 Will[m] Edwards Sloop Ann [from] Connect.
M[r] Johnson Traider
9 Jam[s] Dickey Sloop Lucey from N Carolina
Eliz[h] Carren Wife to an Inhab[t] of Hallifax
Nailer Hatch Sloop Dolphin [from] Hallifax
M[r] Comerin Traider His wife & 2 Children
M[rs] Colmen & 2 Children
10 Tho[s] Simonton Sloop Susanna [from] New F[d] Land
Cap[n] Aaron Vibert & 3 Lads to His Care
Cha[s] M. Roe a Carpenter
16 Cap[n] Benj[a] Hollowey
M[r] Jn[o] Timmins Merch[t]
M[r] Pitman D[o]
M[r] Cobbett D[o]
Rev[d] M[r] Walter
Rev[d] M[r] Frink
Cap[n] Chevelier Marrin[r]
M[r] Brumskett Merch[t]
The above passengers pr Brig[t] Hannah Rob[t] Jervis from London
18 Geo. Derrecott Snow Betsey & Ruth from London
Cap[n] Jam[s] Brett, Cap[n] Jn[o] Polle, Alex[r] Willson, W[m] Phillips, M[r] Samuel — Marriners
M[r] Char[s] Dilley Merch[t]
Tho[s] Mills Carpenter
19 W[m] Morton Brig[e] Industry from Barbados
Rich[d] Miller, Rich[d] Gallispie — Merch[t].
Cap[n] Mastin Marrin[r]
Cap[n] Jos[h] Cordis & 5 Sailors
20 Will[m] Ruggles Sloop Kingston from Hallifax
M[r] Josiah Rose a Docter
John Pirkins Sloop Kittey [from] North Carolina
M[r] Step[n] Harden a Planter
21 Tho[s] Sturgis Sloop Defiance [from] Rh[o] Island.
M[r] Jos[h] Goodwin Merch[t]
23 Jerem[h] Smith Sloop Seaflower from Piscatuqua
Cap[n] Matt[w] Sheaffe
26 Josiah Hubbel Sloop Seaflower [from] Connect[t]
The Rev[d] Edw[d] Winslow & 7 Children
Rob[t] Manderston Snow Douglass from Greenout
Cap James Colhourn, W[m] Marshall, Jn[o] Kennedy, James Paul, Pyem Blowers, Cap Collin Campbell, Malcom Gills, Thom[s] Steel, Jacob Robinson, James Coghran — Marriners

Mr Daniel Dockery } Merchants.
Mr Andw Dalglish
Mr Andw Dalyell
John Robinson Alex Rankin Carpenters
Simon Frasier, Labourer
Patrick McClaran Ditto & his Wife
Patrick McCowan Ditto
Donald Camron Ditto
Wm Reed Millwright & his Wife
John Cameron & Geo Slater Ditto
John Clark Shoemaker
Patrick & Geo Laply Joyners
Aug 6 Benjn Smith Brigt Smith [from] Liverpool
Andw Johnson a Marrinr & His wife
Wm Ringby a Mercht
Wm Caustin & Dudley Swan Marriners
— Aaron Purbeck Sloop Molley from Hallifax
Saml Blagden a Trader
9 John Rea Sloop Polley from North Carolina
Capn Eddy Marrinr
13 Nathl Atwood Sloop Swallow [from] Hallifax
Mr Bird Mercht
Mrs Ray of Hallifax
Joseph Barrett Sloop Nancy from Connectt
Capn Hewen & His Wife
17 Stepn Burroughs Schoonr Mercury from Connectt
Mr Josa Winslow son to the Rev Mr Winslow
20 Jams Deming Sloop Success from Connectt
—— Steward a Labourer
Abigail Brown Spinster
George Vincent Sloop two Sisters from New Fd Land
Capn Jams Ryley & His people
Joshua Aitken Sloop Ann from Scotland
Capn Jno Aitken } Marriners
Jno Law
Jams Drysdale
Jno Herens
Heny Dempenstone
Jno Mainland
Mr John Lewis } Merchts
Mr Jno Fleming
Mr Geo. Lindsey
Edwd Brounett Brigt Favourite from Bristol
Mr Amanuel Elmes Mercht
Capn Thomas
Mr Arthur Prichard a Taylor His Wife & 3 Children
24 Amos Shaffield Sloop Desire from Nova Scotia.
Mr Alliburton a Farmer & Wife
James Thomson Soldier & Wife
Mrs Thomson Wife to a Tailor & 4 Children
Jno Colters a Farmer
David Brace Brigt Polley from New Fd Land
Jno Canturen a Frenchman.

28 Eben[r] Symms Ship Jn[o] Galley [from] S[t] Christophers
Cap[n] Jn[o] Deselvayer Marrin[r] & Wife
Step[n] Seavey Schoon[r] Abig[l] from Piscatuqua
Geo Homans —— Parsons Taylors
2 Sailors Margrett a Spinster.

Sep 3[d] Alex[r] Inglish Brig[t] Salley from Quebec
Connard Smith Baker & Wife
Jn[o] Jones Merch[t]
Jn[o] Collman Trader.
Will[m] Ruggles Sloop Kingston from Hallifax
Jn[o] Burk a Soldier
Sanders West Merch[t]
Amerey Davis Ditto
Peter Young Labourer.
Jn[o] Mackey Brig[t] Nellam [?] from Piscatuqua
Marg[t] & Ann Gardner Spinsters

5 Jam[s] Scott Schoon[r] Frederick from Hallifax
Cap[n] M[c]Neal Marriner.

8 Sam[l] Hinkley Sloop Eliz[th] from Philadelphia
2 Captains of Vessels.

11 Rob[t] M[c]Cordey Schoon[r] Han[h] from Cork & Hallifax
Nath[l] Dangger a Wool Comber
Fran[s] Rien Bookkeeper
Tho[s] Cook James Coffe } Labourers
Morgan Mullons Jam[s] Brien }
M[rs] Dorin Wife to a Labourer of this town & sons
Mary Connell Rich[d] Bourke }
John Costolo Mick[l] Clary }
James Furlong Tim[y] Collens }
John Callahan John Bryen } Servants
John Branfield John Callahan }
Patrick Harden Jam[s] Stewart }
John Reding Benj[n] Davison. }

" Will[m] Maxwell Schoon[r] Nelly from St Johns
Joseph Meremen a Farmer
Rob[t] Basker a Ditto
George Cockran a Ditto & His wife

18 Abner Stocking Schoon[r] Tryal from N. London
M[r] Rich[d] Dudley Merch[t] & Wife

Dup Abner Stocking Schoon[r] Tryal from New London
M[r] Rich[d] Dudley Merch[t] & Wife

20 Eleaz[r] Goodwin Sloop Dobbs from N. Carolina
Cap[n] Rob[t] Jones a Marrin[r]

21 Simon Cooper Sloop Endeavour from Casco Bay
Cap[n] Eph[m] Jones Marrin[r]. Benj[n] Titcomb } Merch[ts]
M[r] Osgood, M[r] Dingle }

" Tho[s] Grinly Schoon[r] Pearl from Granada
John Symms a Bookkeeper

Oct 2[d] Joseph Swansey Sloop Mary from Rh[d] Island
M[rs] Baxter Wife to an Inholder

6 John Junkins Sloop Ranger from S[t] Peters N. F[d] Land
Cap[n] W[m] Albespe Marrin[r]

9 John Renton Schoon$^{r}$ Fly from Liverpool
M$^{r}$ Anderson Tallow Chandler & His Daughter
15 Joseph Chapman Sloop Success from Connect$^{t}$
Jn$^{o}$ Loring Tallow Chandler
John Lillie Ship Thomas from Gaudelope
Char$^{s}$ Bushon a Shoemaker & His Wife
Nehem$^{h}$ Somes Schoon$^{r}$ S$^{t}$ Elizabeth from Philadelphia
Two Farmers names not known
Nath$^{l}$ Atwood Sloop Swallow from Hallifax
List not given in
Sam$^{l}$ Das[h]wood Brig$^{t}$ Deep Bay from London
Sam$^{l}$ Cary Esq.
M$^{r}$ Morley Merch$^{t}$
Tho$^{s}$ Clarke Watchmaker
Nath$^{l}$ Curtis Sloop Nancy from Philadelphia
M$^{r}$ Smith a Farmer
Cap$^{n}$ Will$^{m}$ Albispe Marrin$^{r}$
Rob$^{t}$ Calef Ship London Pack$^{t}$ from London
Col Dyer Comptrol$^{r}$ for New London
M$^{r}$ Geo. Miles D$^{o}$ for New Haven
Ezek$^{l}$ Hersey Merch$^{t}$ Cap$^{n}$ W$^{m}$ Price in 25 Regm.
22 Nath$^{l}$ Curtis Sloop Nancy from Philadelphia
M$^{r}$ Smith a Farmer. [Dup. Entry]
24 Will$^{m}$ Weston Schoon$^{r}$ Jane from Ditto [Philadelphia]
W$^{m}$ Harris Traider
Rob$^{t}$ Tweed D$^{o}$
John Work
Jam$^{s}$ Ryon
—— Blackdoor.
Eben$^{r}$ Gorham Brig$^{t}$ Mairmaid from Kirkwell
W$^{m}$ Fredrick Mankey Merch$^{t}$
31 John Robertson Snow Providence from London
Isabel Baird, Hellen Morison, Jean Munroe } Maid Servts.
M$^{r}$ Smith Merch$^{t}$ & Wife & 3 Children
M$^{r}$ Cort Merch$^{t}$ His wife & 1 child
Cap$^{n}$ Talham, M$^{r}$ Waddy } Marrin$^{s}$
Rob$^{t}$ Calder, John Hume, W$^{m}$ Martin, W$^{m}$ Brown, W$^{m}$ Harling, Alex$^{r}$ Donnald } Serv$^{ts}$
M$^{r}$ Robertson
Benoni Smith Ship Prince of Wales from London
Cap$^{n}$ Jn$^{o}$ Maxwell & Serv$^{t}$
Lew$^{s}$ Primrose for Cannady
Nov Jam$^{s}$ Dickey Sloop Lucy for Annapolis
Rev$^{d}$ M$^{r}$ Rice & Sister
Doct Hartshorne

Lydia Sherman Spinster
Thos Clouse Farmer
Jno Souden Do
Caleb Brooks Do
Sarah Whitherhead
Josep Swan Schoonr Squid from New Fd Land
List not given in.
Ailas [Silas] Atkins Schoonr Dolphen Ditto
List not given in
Hugh McPhilomy Sloop Betsey Ditto
List not given in.
7 Willm Cochren Sloop Neptune Do
List not given in.
20 Abel Badger Sloop America [from] Philadelphia
Mr Chasley [?] a Goldsmith
John Waterman Sloop Deborah [from] Philadelphia
Moses Black a Youth for Education.
26 Danl Waters Brigt Peggy from N. Fd Land
Jams Thompson Traider
Wm Pike Fisherman
Geo Mitchel Sloop Molley from Annapolis
Jonn Church
Jonn Larrance
Saml Read
Jonn Farnsworth } Farmers
Obed Butler
John Dyer
Chas Hall.
Captain Silas Atkins List now sent.
Dec 3 Willm Brock Sloop Anson for Philadelphia
Mr Wilson a Traider
6 John Doubleday Schoonr Industry from Mounte Cristo
Joseph Newell a Cooper & His son.
Heny Atkins Sloop Grayhound [from] New Fd Land
Capn Wm Moor
Capn Archer —— a servt
a Sergant his name not givin in
8 Simeon Freeman Sloop Elizth from Connectt
a Molato Servt to Mr Parmer.
Seth Jenkins Sloop Bristol from Philadelphia
Mr Owen a Marriner.
13 Eleazr Goodwin Sloop Dobbs for N. Caroa
Mr Chandler a Marrinr
Willm Sheppard Sloop Polley [from] N. Fd Land
Mrs Mary —— Widow
Capn Cavenough Marrinr.
27 John Robinson Brigt Freemason from Cork
John Lyon a Clergyman for Taunton
John Bowden a Ensign for New York
Eleonor Benson for Ditto
Ann Segerson & Son for Philada
Richd Burk a Servt

Math$^{w}$ M$^{c}$Namara
John Roberts
David Howe a Phisit$^{n}$
Armiger Howe a Marrin$^{r}$
Malak$^{y}$ Field
John Cleary a Baker
Jam$^{s}$ Brown a Coachman
Edw$^{d}$ Moor a Carpenter
John Moor a Serv$^{t}$
W$^{m}$ Dunavaz a Blacksmith
Martin Dunavan Ditto
And$^{w}$ Barrett, Catharine Lynch, Mary Dunavan, Mary Dresden } Servants.

**1765.**

Jan$^{y}$ 9 Nath$^{l}$ Atwood Sloop Swallow from Hallifax.
M$^{r}$ Barthol$^{y}$ Kneeland Merch$^{t}$
Cap$^{n}$ Broadstreet
Abrah$^{m}$ Rogers a Carpenter
M$^{r}$ Molliken a Sugar Baker & Wife
John Francis a Carpenter
Eliz$^{th}$ Wall to Cap$^{n}$ Phillips of the Castle
Patrick Kerrel a Traider.

Feb 27 David Child Scoon$^{r}$ Tryal from South Carrolina
Cap$^{n}$ W$^{m}$ Waters Marrin$^{r}$ & Boy

Mar 11 Sam$^{l}$ Sampson Sloop Charm$^{g}$ Sally [from] Hallyfax
Joseph Simpson a Traider

18 Jn$^{o}$ Renton Schoon$^{r}$ Fly from Georga
M$^{r}$ Kerwood a Merch$^{t}$

" Nath$^{l}$ Atwood Sloop Swallow from Hallifax
Jn$^{o}$ M$^{c}$Daniel Fisherman Rob$^{t}$ Carrel Merch$^{t}$
W$^{m}$ Lambart Sailmaker Nath$^{l}$ Gallop Farmer
Tho$^{s}$ Joslin Ditto Dan$^{l}$ Harvey a Ditto
John Russell His Wife & Child
Mary Lewes & child
Lieut Isway Aldridge
Henry Green a Merch$^{t}$.

25 Jam$^{s}$ Dickey Sloop Lucy from Fort Cumberland
Jon$^{th}$ Baker. Benj$^{n}$ Cull. Jn$^{o}$ Fling. Tho$^{s}$ Collins. Gideon Smith Nehem$^{h}$ Ward Abel Danks } Farmers
M$^{rs}$ Chuse Wife to a Farmer & child.

29 John McKeil Schoon$^{r}$ Betsey from Maryland.
Joseph Boyes Marrin$^{r}$

30 Moses Peirce Sloop Susan$^{a}$ from Connect$^{t}$
Mary Stone belong to Beverly
Justus Taylor Sloop 3 Partners from Rh$^{o}$ Isl$^{d}$
M$^{r}$ Boodey Sold$^{r}$ & Wife
M$^{r}$ Baker Wife to a Goldsmith
M$^{rs}$ Gardner Widow belong to Boston & Daughter

3 gentlemen belonging to Philadelphia
names not yit givin in.

April 5 Rob. Caleff Ship London Pacquet [from] London
Capt John Lyall Marriner.

15 Josiah Goreham Sloop America [from] Philadelphia
Mr Briggs a Student at the Jersey College
Wm Wyer Scoor Grace [from] N. Carrolina
Capn Wm Cockran
Doctr Huns

17 John Dean Brig Kingston [from] Jamaica
Mr Alexr Campbell a Genn

19 Hector Mc Neill Sloop Phenix from Hallyfax
Mr Beardsley Engineer his Wife one child & servant
Mrs Maxwell Wife to Cap Maxwell & 2 children
Mr Martin Pelut a Frenchman
John Godard a Butcher
Peter Young Trader
Phillip Hill Sailor
Mr Saunders belonging to the 40th Regiment
Laurance Dutton Trader
Mr Dumont Butcher
Mr Pepper & Wm Linkletter Sailors

20 Nathl Gardner Scoonr Phenix [from] Philadelphia
Wm Harris, Cha. Cameron, Archd Cunningham } Traders
Edmd Warren Scoonr Sally Connecticut
Fran Price Marriner
Wm Wills Sloop Huldah [from] Connecticut
Nehemh Fisher Peter Halluk Marriners
David Spark Shoemaker.

May 9 Wm Furnell Schoonr Betsey from Piscatiqua
Mr Homan a Taylor
Nathl Patten Sloop Polley from N. Carolina.
Capn Watts Marrinr.
Wm Harper Sloop Speedwell from New York
Mr Dowing Marrinr
Edmd Morton Schoonr Dove from Philada
Mr Gray, Mr Caloon, John Ervin Traiders
John Patten Sloop Susanna ——
Jams Ryan a Labourr

13 Leach Harris Sloop Hampton from So Carolina
Miss Mary Beals a Spinster.
Jams Stillson Schoonr Charmg Molley [from] N. Carolina
Mr Jams Murrey Genm His Wife & Servt
Miss Hannah Clark a Spinster

14 James Stuart Sloop Good Intent from Maryland
Mr Edwd Rutland Mercht
Josiah McNeal a Taylor

16 Saml Skinner Sloop Nancy for Maryland
Joshua Clarke Mercht

May 17 Nathl Atwood Sloop Swallow from Hallifax

Cap^n Peter Trail & Wife
Miss Han^h Peters } Spinsters
Miss Betsey Butters }
Rob^t Cairel Merch^t
John Phagin Ditto
Char^s Green Ditto
Jonath^n Fuite Merch^t
20 Geo. Mitchel Sloop Charm^g Molley from Anapolis
Dan^l Moor Shoemaker His Wife & 4 children
Patty Sprowl a Spinster
Lieut Johnson of the Artill^y
Elisha Hinman Sloop two Friends from Connect^t
Rich^d Coit a Lad for Education.
John Marshall Ship Boston, Packet from London
Cap^n Logie Marrin^r
Serv^t to John Hancock Esq.
James Scott Brig^t Lydia from Ditto [London]
M^r Thom^s Hargraves Gentlem^n
Tho^s Bond Jos^h Smith } Marrin^r
Tho^s Comas Char^l Lepine }
W^m Davis Ship Thomas from Ditto [London]
Cap^n Studson Peter Jones Marrin^r
Rich^d Southcut Snow W^m & Mary from Bristol
Cap^n W^m King Cap^n Thom^s Orin Marrin^rs
Isaac Mathews Brig^t Squaril from Ditto [Bristol]
Cap^n W^m Francis Cap^n Dan^l Codner Marrin^rs
Robert Jervis Brig^t Hannah from London
Cap^n Thom^s Robson Marrin^r
M^r Lewis Chapron Merch^t
23 Sam^l Pirkins Sloop Hepzebath from Providence
Cap^n Bryant } Marrin^s
Sam^l Lovel }
23^d Sam^l Hinkley Sloop three Friends from Philad^a
M^rs Moor a Widow & two Daughters
M^r Killbreath a Traider
Edw^d Bacon Sloop Defiance from Rh^o Island
John & Mickel Boys serv^ts to Cap^n English
31 Tim^y Mix Sloop William from Connect^t
M^rs Grace Lane Wife to a Sailor
Sam^l Snow Schoon^r Molley from Annapolis
David Felch a Farmer
Rich^d Kelley Ditto
John Cowers & His son.
June 3 Jam^s Ford Sloop Rainbow from Hallifax
M^r Dickey Farmer & 3 Children
M^r Robertson Ditto
Eben^r Wales Traider M^r Bly a Hatter
M^r Calef Taylor W^m Peck a Lad for Education
Miss Mary Cowley Spinster
Mary —— a serv^t to M^r McCarrel
4 Caleb Weaver Sloop Industry [from] Dominico
Cap^n M^cGroth Commander of One of His Majestys Ships.

7 Nath$^{l}$ Sherburn Brig$^{t}$ Betsey from Antigua.
Cap$^{n}$ Nathen Steward Marrin$^{r}$
11 Dan$^{l}$ M$^{c}$Carty Ship Salley from Dominico.
M$^{r}$ Geo Ervin
12 Tho$^{s}$ Dixey Brig$^{t}$ Pill Packet from London
John Grimes, George Grimes Seamen
David Dunken, Alex$^{r}$ Dunken.
John Morris, John Christy,
James Silver.
16 Step$^{n}$ Andrews Sloop Dolphen [from] N. Carrolina
W$^{m}$ Cole Merchan$^{t}$
June 16 Abner Stocking Schoon$^{r}$ Ruby from Connect$^{t}$
M$^{r}$ Dan$^{l}$ Fuller }
M$^{r}$ Phelps } Clergymen from Nova Scotia
John Mollony Schoon$^{r}$ Nancy [from] Hallifax
John Lush a Farmer
W$^{m}$ Giles a Hatter & 3 Seamen.
[Dup Entry] Abner Stocking Schoon$^{r}$ Ruby from Conn$^{t}$
M$^{r}$ Dan$^{l}$ Fuller } Clergymen
M$^{r}$ Philps } for Nova Scotia
Christian Higgins Sloop Ruby from Connect$^{t}$
John Minzey Jun & Wife }
John Minzey & W$^{m}$ Minzey } Carpenters
W$^{m}$ Fogue Schoon$^{r}$ Laurance from Annopolis
M$^{rs}$ Anna Phillips & Margery Wilkins her serv$^{t}$
Dan$^{l}$ Davison & His two children
Benj$^{n}$ Fallis & His sister
M$^{rs}$ Mote & Her child.
June 26 Elisha Glover Schoon$^{r}$ Hannah from Nova Scotia
John Logen His wife & 2 children
Char$^{s}$ Cocks Josh. Moor, Dan$^{l}$ Calf Marriners
M$^{rs}$ Steward, M$^{rs}$ Folkner & Child Wives to Farmers
Elijah Bent, Farmer, Caty Macklentick
Alden Bass Brig$^{t}$ Themes from Granada
M$^{r}$ Peter Roe Dalton Merch$^{t}$
Cap$^{n}$ James Brown Mariner
28 Peter Rogers Sloop Polley [from] Connecticut
Cap$^{n}$ Lucas a Marrin$^{r}$ & His Wife.
29 Moses Freeman Sloop Abig$^{l}$ from Georga
M$^{r}$ Teal Clergyman
Sam$^{l}$ Whitney }
Hen$^{y}$ Mills } Merch$^{ts}$
July 1 Josiah Gorham Sloop America from Philadelphia
Rob$^{t}$ Gray Merch$^{t}$
W$^{m}$ Sheward Ditto
M$^{rs}$ Deborah Forder wife to a Ropemaker & 2 Children N. B. Mr. Benj$^{a}$ Austin became answerable to the Selectmen for Mrs Forders & Children
2 Tim$^{y}$ Parker Sloop three Friends from Philadelphia
Archab$^{d}$ Cunningham Merch$^{t}$
W$^{m}$ Kid Do
John Smith Do

John Moor Do [Merch$^{t}$]
Joseph Pumroy a Prisoner
4 James Dickey Sloop Lucy from Fort Cumberland
Cap$^{n}$ Bruce Engineer & four Serv$^{ts}$
Joshua Cozwerse a Butcher
Eliz$^{th}$ Patten a Spinster
M$^{rs}$ Vardy Wife to Sam$^{l}$ Vardy & 2 children
M$^{rs}$ Miller wife to Alex$^{r}$ Miller & 2 children
8 John Molony Schoon$^{r}$ Polley from N. Carolina
Cap$^{n}$ Towers Marriner
14 Joseph Howell Schoon$^{r}$ Peggy from Halifax
M$^{r}$ Jerem Daley Merch$^{t}$ & His wife
15 Nehem$^{h}$ Somes Schoon$^{r}$ Eliz$^{th}$ from Hallifax
M$^{r}$ Wales a Butcher
M$^{r}$ Scarborough a Farmer
M$^{r}$ Harvey a Soldier
M$^{rs}$ Nuttage wife to M$^{r}$ Nuttage & 3 children
— John Bradford Sloop Ginger from Virginia
M$^{r}$ Charles Peal a Painter
16 W$^{m}$ Vernon Schoon$^{r}$ Brittania from Barbados
M$^{r}$ Sam$^{l}$ Sager, Merch$^{t}$
18 Nath$^{l}$ Atwood Sloop Swallow from Hallifax
Miss Mercy Parsons Spinster
Edward Crawley Esq
John Hill Merch$^{t}$
John M$^{c}$Cannon Marriner
Thom$^{s}$ Homer Sloop Eliz$^{th}$ from Hallifax
Fredrick Wasenfelt Merch$^{t}$
Thom$^{s}$ Wilkey Marriner
Laha MackIntash a Soldier
Miss Sarah Guppey Spinster
20 James Roberts Schoon$^{r}$ Betsey [from] North Carolina
M$^{r}$ Skinner Merch$^{t}$.
Thom$^{s}$ Fish Sloop New Polley [?] from Ditto [North Carolina]
W$^{m}$ Fellows Marriner.
23 Caleb Hopkins Schoon$^{r}$ Mary [from] Martinico
Jam$^{s}$ Flood Cooper
David McCloud Marriner
26 Abel Badger Scoon$^{r}$ Eliz. [from] N. Found Land
List not givin in
31 Peter Doyle Brig Sibella [from] N. Found Land
Cap$^{n}$ Carthwright. a Marriner.
— John Blake Ship John Galley from London
Coll Ingersoll & Serv$^{t}$
Rev$^{d}$ M$^{r}$ Eph$^{m}$ Avery
Cap Thom$^{s}$ Lee }
Cap Brown } Marriners
Cap Young }
M$^{r}$ Dishon & M$^{r}$ Dorson Merch$^{ts}$
M$^{r}$ Roberts Joyner
W$^{m}$ Proice a Lad for Education.

31 Thom Sturgis Sloop Defiance [from] R. Island
Jn° Nation Marriner
James Morrison Baker
M^r Halliburton, Farmer
M^rs Thomas wife to a Carphenter at R. Island
Aug 1 Elisha Tower Sloop Unity [from] N. Carrolina
Cap Jn° Simpson a Merch^t his Wife & one child
W^m Wimble Sloop Stamford [from] N. York
M^r W^m Johnson a Gentle^m
Sarah Churchill & 2 Children
2 Edw^d Morton Scoon^r Dove [from] N. Carrolina
M^r Rich^d Veneble a Gen^m
M^r W^m Field Marrin^r
M^r . . . . . . Trader.
3 Sam Pain Sloop Ranger from Maryland
M^r Benj^n Bagnell jun^r Clockmaker
[Dup. ent.] Edmund Morton Schoon^r Dove from N. Carolina
M^r Rich^d Venebel Gentleman
M^r W^m Fields Marriner
A Trader His name not given in.
[Dup. ent.] Sam^l Pain Sloop Ranger from Maryland
M^r Benj^n Bagnell Clockmaker
10 Josiah Gorham Sloop America from Philadelphia
John Hysir a Trader
11 James Barnes Brig^t William from New Castle
Cap^n John Hunt Wendell Marrin^r & His Mate
12 Joseph Sewell Sloop Eliz^th from Granada
M^r John Darbadge Merch^t
Nath^l Patten Sloop Polley from N. Carolina
Cap^n And^w Smith Marrin^r.
20 And^w Sigourney Schoon^r John & Mary from St Eustatia
Doct Spring
M^r Barroc a French Merch^t
Thomas Asburn Ship John from Liverpool
Chris^t Kennedy Cooper & Wife
Juda Duggin a Spinster
John Kelley Cooper & Wife
M^r John Stort Merch^t
22 John Aitken Ship Jemerson & Peggy from Leith
James Dussaale, John Leslie, Rich^d Hamilton, Peter Douglass, Jam^s Calden, Alex^r Ramage, Roger Ballingall, Rob^t Lawson, Alex Ross, James Crombie, James Wilson, Peter Ternie, Alex^r Ballingall } Marriners
Cap^n Rob^t Scott an Officer
John Wood wife & 2 Children a Farmer
Will^m Vitch, Rob^t Nisbett, Thom^s Scott } Labourers

Sir Henry Seaton
Will^m^ Blair Merch^t^
John M^c^Master Ditto
Alex^r^ Ferbes Printer & Wife
James Archibald Ditto
Will^m^ Taylor & Lad.
24 Aaron Purbuck Sloop Kingstone from New York
Abraham Mathews a Labourer
[Dup. ent.] Thom^s^ Ashburn Ship John from Liverpool
Christop^r^ Kennedy a Cooper & Wife
John Kelly a Ditto & Wife
Juda Duggin a Spinster
M^r^ John Stort Merch^t^.
28 Abner Homes Schoon^r^ Sally from New Providence
M^r^ —— Bradford Merch^t^
James Ford Sloop Dolphen from Hallifax
Larrance Nutson Trader
And^w^ Acher Ditto
Mich^l^ M^c^Nemaro Ditto
M^r^ M^c^Carty Ditto
Elisha White Sloop Tryal from Connect^t^
M^r^ Burrel } Shoemakers
M^r^ Mansfield }
29 Seth Doan Sloop Polley from Connecticut
John Bond a Marriner
Nath^l^ Rogers a Lad to the care of M^r^ Thomas Sail-maker
30 John Doubleday Schoon^r^ Industry from N. Carolina
M^r^ Corn^s^ Gooningdike Merch^t^
Tim^y^ Parker sloop 3 Friends from Philadelphia
Step^n^ Davis }
James Davis } Marriners
Nailer Marriner }
Sept 2 Eben^r^ Ledyard Sloop Hannah from Connect^t^
M^rs^ Baldwin a Widow
3 Leach Harris Schoon^r^ Sibella from Barbados
M^r^ Anthony Coverly Merch
4 Will^m^ Fuggo Schoon^r^ Dove from Annapolis
Tabothy Tomlinson Sert to Cap^n^ Foggo
5 Nehem^h^ Somes Schoon^r^ Eliz^th^ from Hallifax
Joseph Foster Mason
Nath^l^ Belknap Seaman
John Sag Trader
W^m^ Barmalyne Doctor
John Shores Fisherman
Sackwell Pearide Yeoman
Aggash Newman Trader
Eben^r^ Wells Ditto
M^rs^ Winslow & children
M^rs^ Prescot
M^rs^ Loller
Miss Vans

Mrs Miller
Saml Rogers Sloop Betsey [from] New Fd Land
Edwd Pool Wm Keen
Con Casey John Strurd } Seamen
John Simons
7 John Waterman Sloop Deborah [from] Philadelphia
Mr Gray a Trader
10 Robt Wier Sloop Phenix from Quebec
Thoms Weams
Saml Beard } Lawyers
Capn Robt Leutt (?) Marriner
11 Jams Montgomerie Ship Douglis [from] Liverpool
Capn Thoms Shearman 2 Seamen & a Boy
Wm Deverson Ship Thomas & Samuel from London
George Meserve Esq
Doct Lincoln
Mr Wm Gore a Mercht
Mr Dexter a Smith
Mr Jams Bugenan a Farmer & Wife
12 Anthy Fletcher Schoonr three Friends from Maryland
Mr Saml Shelton Sloss a Mercht
13 Simeon Freeman Sloop Success from N. Carolina
John Pitman for Education.
Joseph Rotch Schoonr Diamond from Philadelphia
Thoms Bell, Robt Bell, John Harkless
Robt Willey, Willm Gort, John Murey } Labourers
Joanes Young, Mercy Morrey — Spinsters.
16 Alexr Gorden Schoonr Fancy [from] North Carolina
Thoms Cooper Mercht
Heny Locker — Ditto
21 Isaac Belnap Schoonr Newbury from N. York
Mr George a Sugar Baker
Nathl Atwood Sloop Swallow from Hallifax
Mrs Mary Clap & Her Servt. Mrs Hollons & 2 Children
Elizth Murphy for Quebec
Joshua French, Phillip Kermont, Josh Cook
Wm Williamson, Peter Ryon, Capn Dickey. } Traders
Godfrey Contestine, John Clark, Ebenr Silsbey
Bartho Pecker, Jno Rock, Ebenr Switcher, Davd Crafton, Carpenters
23 Corns Annabel Sloop Gull from Cape Sable
Mrs Doble Wife to Capn Doble
Mr Collins of Cape Cod & Wife.
Mrs Pereway of Liverpool Nova Scotia
26 Robt Davis Ship Blizard from Antigua
Thos Oliver Esq Gentlemen & 2 Servts
Mr Wm. Cowthorn Mercht
30 Thoms Hulme Ship Jno Galley from London
The Revd Willm Augar
Capn Jno Mills

Oct. 1 Jon[th] Pierpoint Sloop Ranger from Hallifax
M[r] Sam[l] Guild Butcher
M[r] Thom[s] Cashman Smith
2 David Shand Snow Tristram from London
Cap[n] Moses Wingate Marriner
M[r] Charles Oliver Dubolia } French Gentlemen
M[r] —— Derrigrand } for Hallifax
8 Isaac Smith Schoon[r] Dolphen from Philadelphia.
Will[m] Bennett a Hatter
3 Sailors
Tim[y] Parker Sloop 3 Friends from Philadelphia
Dan[l] Doler a Goldsmith
Will[m] Weston Sloop Union from Philadelphia
M[r] Jesse Maris a Trader.
9 Silas Atkins Schoon[r] Dolphen from N. F[d] Land
W[m] Dean Eben[r] Flower, John Mackroth
Mich[l] Morse, Eben[r] Hinkley, Dan[l] Bridges, }
John Lakey, Will[m] Shaw, W[m] Corby, } Marri-
Sadaros Thorn, John Wallis, Rich[d] Parater, } ners
Roger Warnall, John Torner, W[m] Halse. }
10 Samuel Doggett Sloop Commerce from N. Carrolina
M[r] Tisdal a Merch[t] & his Daughter
14 Joseph White Sloop Eagle from N. Carrolina
Cap[n] Peirson }
Cap[n] Crandon } Marriners
W[m] Smith }
W[m] Cockran Scoon[r] Lawrence from N. Found Land
John Thurston, Tim[th] Cotterill, Josh[a] Cadole, }
Sam Davis, Jere[h] Roles, Joseph Bartlett, }
Thom[s] Brigs James Trefary, John Durk, }
J. — Owen, John Nettleton, Jn[o] Herrington, }
David Smith, Jn[o] Dennie, Jn[o] Gilroy, } Fisher-
Joseph Snellum, W[m] Hannon, Jn[o] Ore, } man &
Hen[y] Bosworth, Patrick Conner, Leon[d] Baily, } Marri-
Charles Sharpley, Jarius Fulls, Valt Conner, } ners
Tho[s] Borden, Patrick Dutting, Jerem[h] Haley, }
Jn[o] Brockington, Dennis Roian, Edw[d] Waddy, }
Patrick Nuff, Cap[n] Hayman a Marriner & Mr }
Johnson }
19 Noah Hatch Sloop Sarah from Hallyfax
Rob[t] Airy a Farmer
M[r] Goat } Merch[t]
M[r] Hill }
W[m] Randall Printer
John Shan Shoemaker
W[m] Carey Marriner
John ——— a Tobacconist.
21 Abner Briggs Sloop Deborah from Nantucket
M[rs] Smith a Widow She came from London to Nantucket.
Rob[t] Hunter Ship Devonshire from London
Cap George Willson

Cap Jn$^{o}$ Langdon
Rob$^{t}$ Lamberth a Taylor & His wife.
A maiden servt. to Mr. Vassall

22 Shubal Coffin Scoon$^{r}$ Hawk from London
M$^{r}$ George Malson [?]
Cap$^{n}$ Constant Freeman a Marriner
M$^{rs}$ Sawyer a Widow belonging to Newbury

24 Benj$^{n}$ Green Schoon$^{r}$ Nova Scotia from Hallifax
Cap$^{n}$ Preston Officer in His Majesties Service
Benj$^{n}$ Gerrish Esq His Wife & Daughter & Servant
M$^{r}$ William Smith Merch$^{t}$
M$^{r}$ James Forrist Ditto
Malu$^{h}$ Salter Jun for Education.

25 Elisha Glover Schoon$^{r}$ Charm$^{g}$ Hannah from Nova Scotia

| | | |
|---|---|---|
| David Long, | David Cutten | Farmers |
| W$^{m}$ M$^{c}$Clintick | Will$^{m}$ Day | |
| John Davis, John Brook, Patrick Dowing | | |
| John Willson | Samuel Potter | |

Mrs Folknor, Eliz$^{th}$ Andrews Spinster

28 Peter Doyle Brig$^{t}$ Sebella from New F$^{d}$ Land

| | | |
|---|---|---|
| Thom$^{s}$ Keeffs | John Shannahan | Fishermen & Seamen |
| Edmond Weeken | Patrick Herrin | |
| Edmond Barret | Thom$^{s}$ Downs | |
| John Ryan | Thom$^{s}$ Keoho | |

Mary Bleake Ann Bleake Servants
David Welch Thom$^{s}$ Linch Seamen

Moses Roach Schoon$^{r}$ Squid from New F$^{d}$ Land.

| | | |
|---|---|---|
| W$^{m}$ Cummins | Jam$^{s}$ Cambell | Marriners |
| Rob$^{t}$ Sample | Jn$^{o}$ Galpin | |
| John Larey | Corn$^{s}$ Nophen | |
| John Bryan | Math$^{w}$ Kelley | |
| Math$^{w}$ Ginsford | Math$^{w}$ Knight | |
| Jn$^{o}$ Burk | Jn$^{o}$ Flannagin | |
| Jn$^{o}$ Cunningham | Jn$^{o}$ Melledge | |
| Corn$^{s}$ Perry | Jam$^{s}$ Tucklen | |
| Step$^{n}$ Fosdick | Will$^{m}$ Lassey | |
| Tho$^{s}$ Roach | Jn$^{o}$ Callahan | |

Tho$^{s}$ Mitchel Schoon$^{r}$ Mary from New F$^{d}$ Land
Math$^{w}$ Tarber, Jon$^{a}$ Steel } Fishermen.

31 Dan$^{l}$ Malcom Sloop Rose from Hallifax
W$^{m}$ Doyde Merch$^{t}$

Nov 4 Benj$^{n}$ Cob Sloop Salley from Quebec
Wil$^{m}$ Edwards Serv$^{t}$ to M$^{r}$ Martin Gay
Mick$^{l}$ Malcom to the care of Cap$^{n}$ Malom

Solomon Bangs Sloop Desire from Philadelphia
M$^{r}$ Tho$^{s}$ Batt Shoemaker

Mungo Mackay Brig$^{t}$ Polley from New Castle
Cap$^{n}$ Sam$^{l}$ Bulfinch Marrin$^{r}$

Sam$^{l}$ Gray Schoon$^{r}$ Rainbow from New F$^{d}$ Land
Sam$^{l}$ Sheppard John Spering.

Tho$^{s}$ Hutchinson — Jos. Raymond
Jn$^{o}$ Lamm — Rob$^{t}$. Saunders
Jn$^{o}$ Kavanaugh — Sam. Pepper
Lewis Parrott — Jn$^{o}$ Farnam
Jn$^{o}$ Marshall — Jn$^{o}$ Nations
Edw$^{d}$ Leores — Eben$^{r}$ Lane
W$^{m}$ Thurston — Helton Stevens
Mich$^{l}$ M$^{c}$Namara — Isaac Harkell
Jn$^{o}$ Collinson — Tho. Waterman.

6 Step$^{n}$ Smith Schoon$^{r}$ Eliz$^{th}$ from Port Rico
Dan$^{l}$ Fox Merch$^{t}$

9 Elisha Crocker Sloop Dolphin from Hallifax
John Hunt Ebenz$^{r}$ Wallis — Traders
Jam$^{s}$ Morgan, Jn$^{o}$ Murphey, Nich$^{s}$ Poor, John M$^{c}$Grah — Fishermen

11 Isaac Phillips Sloop Nancy from New F Land
M$^{r}$ O'Neal Merch$^{t}$ & His Serv$^{t}$.
Edward Moor, Corn$^{s}$ Mahan, Silvest Cambell, Rich$^{d}$ Butler, Tho$^{s}$ Ring, Patrick Dallany, Jam$^{s}$ Crary, Luke Shanton, Joseph Port, Jn$^{o}$ Crow, Rob$^{t}$ West, Rich$^{d}$ Stafford, Will$^{m}$ Williams — Fishermen.

12 Abner Stocking Schoon$^{r}$ Tryal from Connect$^{t}$
Katharine Gwin Wife to a Marriner.
James Dickey Sloop Lucy from Nova Scotia
David Seckett, Rob$^{t}$ Danks, Thom$^{s}$ Clues, Jn$^{o}$ Sullivan & Wife, Oliver Pratt, M$^{r}$ Esbent, Joseph Kent, Eben$^{r}$ Bates, Benj$^{n}$ How, Jam$^{s}$ King, Terence King, Joseph Willet, Nath$^{l}$ Fisher, Fran$^{s}$ Keyne, Nich$^{s}$ Starr (?) — Farmers

13 Nath$^{l}$ Atwood Sloop Swallow from Halifax
M$^{rs}$ Hannah Bean a Widow & her child
Ruth Harris wife to a Boat Builder & child
George King a Merch$^{t}$
Joseph Wilson & Sam Bleigh Hatters
W$^{m}$ Dean Marriner. Joshua Franch, Eli Snow
Jno Bryant, James Wallis Mich$^{l}$ Flanegin
David Denney, George Lumbert — Sailors

---

Dennis Skinner — Math Summer
Jn$^{o}$ Lusher — W$^{m}$ Morges
George Kobert — Henry Walter
John Coshell — George Unkester
Deval Shouts — Leonard Cronnig.
Henry Quarks —— Farmers.

18 Benj$^{n}$ Green Jun$^{r}$ Schooner Nova Scotia Packett from Hallifax

Mr Clarkson Mr Pettett Mr Jacobs Mr Wain
Mr Caton Gentn belonging to Philadelphia
Lieutenant Crosby Mr Henry Deering Mercht
Richard Abrahams & his wife & Daughter a Trader
John Coppinger Sloop Phenix from Quebeck.
Capt Saml Sinkler
20 Stephen Emery Sloop Seaflower from Louisburg
John Pendergrass & Thomas ——— Fishermen
25 Daniel Waters Brigt Peggy & Hannah from Tortola
Capn James Ryadon a Marriner.
Stepn Hayter schoonr Kittey from Madgilen
Michl Carney & Wife
Morris Garrey & Wife
Richd Morgen — Charles Dorren
Jams Poor senr     Jams Poor jur
Jereml Folley     Timy Nuton
Edmund Coflin     John McGee
Geo Fizpatrick     Richd Luby
27 Saml Pirkens Sloop Hephzibath from New Providence
Capn Nathl Williams & 4 of His Sailors
Mrs Elizth Baker a Widow
29 Heny Atkins Schoonr Dolphen from New F Land.
Capn Lilly & 2 servants.
Richd Hamblen Brigt Wolf from the Orkney Island
Geo. Crag Mercht.
Dec 9 Thos Mathews Sloop Success from N. Fd Land
Capn Field & 6 Sailors
Linsford Morey Schoonr Jannet from ye Island St Johns
John Foot Isaac Lawrance Fishermen
[?] Alex } Aloz } Donnel, Cooper
James Williston Blacksmith
David Sullivan Fisherman
11 Willm Damerell Sloop Hope from N. Fd Land
Josh Quin - Fisherman
David Livey - Sailor
12 John Foweraker Scoonr Apprentice from N. F. Land
Mr Richd Waterman a Trader
Mr Peter Prim a Mercht
Fra Tree Sloop Chamg Molly from N. F. Land
Capt Bass & three Sailors
16 James Scott Brig Lydia from London
Mrs Bedford wife to Capn Bedford at New York
Mr Nath Potter.     Mr Benj Roberts } Gentlemen
Mr Andw Mack     Mr Thoms Coleman } Gentlemen
Mr John Allen
Mr Justice Jeremh Gager of Connecticut
Andw Stewarth Servt to Majr Rogers.
Dec 23 John Whitmarsh Scoonr Dove from Philadelphia
Mr Wm Sweat.
Elisha Tower Sloop Unity from N. Carrolina

Cap$^{n}$ Alex$^{r}$ Smith a Marriner.
W$^{m}$ Davis Ship Thomas from London
Cap Isaac Casneau, Cap$^{t}$ Benj$^{a}$ White } Marriners
Cap$^{n}$ Rob$^{t}$ Twicraft }
Paul Schryder a Taylor his Wife & 3 children.
27 James Bruce Ship John & Suckey from London
Doc$^{t}$ Charles Russell
M$^{r}$ Benj$^{a}$ Stoddard a Merch$^{t}$
Cap$^{n}$ Bryant a Marriner
M$^{r}$ John Rufels a Frenchman

**1766.**

Jan 15 Benj Parker Sloop Lovy from Philadelphia
M$^{r}$ Robert Gray }
M$^{r}$ And$^{w}$ M$^{c}$Cullock } Merch$^{ts}$
M$^{r}$ Alex$^{r}$ Hannah }
22 Will$^{m}$ Craig Snow Peggy from Glasgo
Rob$^{t}$ Moody Alex$^{r}$ * . . lbrege Jam$^{s}$ Wilson Merchants
David Iver, Jueler
Humphry M$^{c}$Donald Gentle$^{n}$
Jam$^{s}$ M$^{c}$Donald, Jam$^{s}$ Robison, }
John M$^{c}$Donald, Jam$^{s}$ M$^{c}$Donald, } Husbandmen
Donald M$^{c}$Donald, Hugh Thomson. }
Alex$^{r}$ Wilson, Alex$^{r}$ Ramsey, Jam$^{s}$ Tayler } Sailors
Joseph Elden, Jam$^{s}$ Sutherland }
John Loang, Carpenter
Jerem$^{h}$ Rogers Schoon$^{r}$ Hallifax Packet from Halifax
John Averly, Peter Barr, Fred$^{k}$ Braden Merch$^{ts}$
27 W$^{m}$ Foggo Schoon$^{r}$ Charm$^{g}$ Han$^{h}$ from Añapolis
M$^{r}$ Benj$^{n}$ Ramsey Gentleman
Benj Lee a Lad for Education.
Jan$^{y}$ 29 Step$^{n}$ Swain Schoon$^{r}$ Salley from New Providence
Patrick Mahon Merch$^{ts}$
Sam$^{l}$ Pepper Schoon$^{r}$ Olive Branch from Hallifax
John Harris Boat builder
Jam$^{s}$ Steel a Farmer
Feb 4 Will$^{m}$ Deverson Ship Brittania from London
Cap$^{n}$ George Diamond Marrin$^{r}$
M$^{r}$ James Waller Merch$^{t}$
27 Nath$^{l}$ Atwood Sloop Swallow from Hallifax
M$^{r}$ Jn$^{o}$ Carby Mr Eben$^{r}$ Wales Merch$^{t}$
Gentlemen

I have bought a Girles time that was brought from New Found Land in the Brig$^{t}$ Sebella Peter Doyle Master which You will find Enter'd Octob 25$^{th}$ 1766. I am Your Hum. Sevt Rich$^{d}$ Russell

Mar 13 Jerem$^{h}$ Rogers Schoon$^{r}$ Nova Scotia from Hallifax
Ann & Jane Clarke Spinsters.
22 Paul Jenkins Schoon$^{r}$ Fox from Cape Fear
M$^{r}$ James Nicholes Merch$^{t}$
Tim$^{y}$ Parker Sloop 3 Friends from Philadelphia

Mrs Moor a Widow & Son.
John Witmarsh Schooner Dove from Philadelphia
Wm Murrey Trader & Wife
Chars Comerin Ditto
Wm Dager Ditto.
April 2 Jonth Greely Sloop Susana from St Eustatia.
Capn Lowell of Newbury
5 Andrew Langworth Sloop Dolphen from Rho Island
Mr —— Northup Silk Dyer His wife & 4 Children
Juremh Rogers Schoonr Nova Scotia Packet from Halifax
Doctor Carriwood
Mr John Brinnon Merchts
7 Nailer Hatch Sloop Salley from Hallifax
Mr Wales a Trader.
14 Henry Smith Ship Liberty from Lisbon
Capn Bee Marriner & Boy
Uriel Oakes Schoonr Unity from Louisburg
Mr Diber a Trader
James Cogswell Ditto
John Freeman Seaman
Justus Taylor Sloop three Partners from Connectt
Ashbell Anderson Shoe Maker
His wife sister & 3 children
15 Josiah Burnham Sloop Olive from Connecticut
David Jones Sailmaker
2 Frenchmen Fishermen
16 Jonathn Davis Schoonr Industry from Martineco.
Mr Stepn Montgomery Mercht
Thomas Homes Sloop Ruby from North Carolina
John Nesbet Trader
Howard Jacobson Ship Boscowen from London
Mr Saml Hollowell Mercht
Mr Thoms Nash Gentleman
Mr John Core Ditto
Mrs Abigl Jones beloning to Boston
Mr James Doyle a Trader
Robt Caleb Ship London Packet from London
Capn Chars Chaliver Marrinr
Mr Maul an Ensign.
James Colhourn Ship Sterling Castle from Greenock.
Cap James Malcolm, Cap Jno Ritchie, Cap Heny Hinian, John Morris, Jno Letham, Duncan McLean, Hugh Kell, Andw Crawford, Wm Ramsay — Marriners
John Fisher, Danl Montgomery, Ship Carpenters
John McCarter Flax Dresser
James Connell a School master
John Barcley a Dyer
Lucas Florin, Anthony Dole—Image Makers
Bartholmy Florin.

22 Hugh McLean Scoon[r] John & Jaz from Ireland
Archib[d] Steward James Willson } Marriners.
John Parlin Jn[o] Robinson }
Alex Nichols Jn[o] Newell } Joyners
Rob[t] Hogh }
W[m] Young Alex[r] Willson Weavers
John Stevenson James Lone } Farmers
Will[m] Boyde }
Thomas Safely a Taylor
Patrick Campbell a Piper
Joseph Brooks a Trader
W[m] Higgings a Shoemaker
Hen[y] McKennery a Bleacher.
W[m] Furnell Scoon[r] Betsey from Portsmouth
M[r] John Homans
27 Jacob Goodsill Sloop Charm[g] Hannah from Connecticut
Abrah[m] Foot a Farmer
May 1 Sam Soul Sloop Rainbow from Antigua
Thomas Anthony Marriner
5 Tim[th] Parker Sloop three friends [from] Philadelphia
William Harris Trader
6 James Dickey Scoon[r] free America from Annapolis
M[r] Spragues M[r] King } Farmers
M[r] Webbers }
May 9 Joseph McLallean Scoon Beaver from Antigua
M[r] Edw[d] Smith a Merch[t]
10 John Whitmarsh Scoon[r] Dove from Philadelphia
M[r] John Weatherhead a Merch[t]
M[r] Charles Camerin a Trader.
12 Nathan Swain Scoon[r] Flora from St Christopher
M[r] W[m] Farbeshon } Merch[ts].
M[r] Tarry Owen }
14 Eben[r] Rogers Sloop America from Philadelphia
Belter Manter } Husbandman
Josiah Stilton }
Archabald Crawford Sloop Charm[g] Molley [from] Nova Scotia. Lydia Farnsworth wife to M[r] Farnsworth at Annapolis
Joseph Coin a Frenchman
David Shand Brig[t] Tristam from London
Cap[n] Joseph Hall } Marriners
Cap[n] Alex[r] Smith }
M[r] John Whittaker a Merch[t].
Shuball Coffin Brig Harrison from London
Cap Nathaniel Coffin a Marriner
M[r] Phillip Canot a Merch[t]
M[r] Fran[s] Miller an Ensign.
John Blake Ship John Galley from London
M[r] John Richey a Carpenter
M[r] James Lewis Blockmaker.
21 Josiah Rogers Scoon[r] Eliz from Philadelphia
——— Richardson a Chaisemaker.

21 Nath Atwood Sloop Swallow from Hallyfax
Coll Pringle Two male & Two female servts
Coll Cunningham & four male servts
Capt. Scott a Son a male & female serv[t]s.
Cap[n] Innis & Serv[t]
M[r] James Stillson Trader
M[r] —— Cook a Merch[t]
M[r] —— Wales a Trader
Corn[s.] Fellows Sloop Seaflower from Vigo
Cap Edw[d] Hoptai a Marriner
— John Smith Brig[t] Prosperity from Scotland
Cap[n] Robert Sinclear Marrin[r]
30 Hector M[c]Neal Sloop Fanny from N. Carolina
M[r] Noice Merch[t]
Edmond Morton Schoon[r] Dove from [N. Carolina]
Jacob Shepard Merch[t]
Nath[l] Bowles Marriner
Phenix Frazier Ditto
Levi Gill Hatter & serv[t]
James Roberts Schoon[r] Betsey from N. Carolina
M[r] Wheeler Blacksmith
Thom[s] Prince Sloop Earl of Bute from N. Carolina
Benj[n] Snode a Lad for Education.
June 3 Nath[l] Dunn Brig[t] Rebecca from Mounta Christa
Stephen White a French Lad
Elijah Doubleday Brig[t] Diana from Ditto [Mounta Christa]
Charles Favour a Frenchman & Wife
John Marshall Ship Boston Packet from London
M[r] Herbert Newton a Lieut
M[r] Fran[s] Green Gentlemen
M[r] Will[m] Spooner
M[r] Clarke His Wife & 2 Daughters.
Rob[t] Montgomery Ship George & James from Scotland.
Will[m] McKeen a Mate & 8 sailors belong[g] to a ship at Casco Bay
Alex[r] Lee a Marriner
James Mull } Joiners
Will[m] Arnit } Joiners
M[r] Baker Gentleman & His wife
M[r] Will[m] Kelso Gentleman
John Tuill Mercht
M[rs] Silkrig Wife to M[r] Jam[s] Silkreg Merch[t] & child
5 Tim[y] Parker Sloop three Friends [from] Philadelphia
M[r] Sullendine Pot Ash Maker
Mathias Amos Sailor.
7 Nehem[h] Somes Sloop Dispatch from Hallifax
Jerem[h] Cushing Carpenter
M[rs] Giffin } Their Husbands at Hallifax.
M[rs] Peirce } Their Husbands at Hallifax.
M[rs] Phippeny } Their Husbands at Hallifax.
Mich[l] Bryant Sailmaker & His Wife

Mary Greenleaf went from Boston
Edw$^{d}$ Deacon Merch$^{t}$
Jam$^{s}$ Dunlap Farmer
Tho$^{s}$ Horsey Distiller

| | | |
|---|---|---|
| Tim$^{y}$ Conner, | Tim$^{y}$ Ratcliff, | Irish servants |
| Peter Larey, | Sam$^{l}$ Davis, | consigned to Mr. |
| Jam$^{s}$ Tool, | Mich$^{l}$ Neal. | Rob$^{t}$ Hallowell |

John Clarke Ship Industry from London
Cap$^{n}$ Sam$^{l}$ Newell Marrin$^{r}$
10 Paschal N. Smith Sloop Speedwell from N. York
John Nevil Thom$^{s}$ Grafton Sailors
John Smith Glover
12 Thom$^{s}$ Hutchings Schoon$^{r}$ Salley from Bermuda
M$^{r}$ Benj$^{n}$ Pemberton Merch$^{t}$ & Wife
M$^{r}$ John Harris Merch$^{t}$ & Son
M$^{r}$ Rich$^{d}$ Hill Planter
M$^{r}$ Jam$^{s}$ Mason Clarke to M$^{r}$ Pemberton
Nath$^{l}$ Porter Sloop Industry from Georga
W$^{m}$ Dunham, Thom$^{s}$ Gibbens — Youths for Education.
13 Moses Peirce Sloop Susanna from Connecticut
4 Sailors belonging to a Vessel at Casco Bay
Elnathan Jones Schoon$^{r}$ Betsey from Martineco
Cap$^{n}$ Joshua Stone & Brother Marriners.
16 Tho$^{s}$ Cartwright Ship Dartmouth from Bristol
M$^{r}$ Will$^{m}$ Jones Merch$^{t}$
Cap$^{n}$ Welchman Marriner
James Newton Spanill Schoon$^{r}$ Unity from Nova Scotia
M$^{r}$ Rob$^{t}$ Stevenson Merch$^{t}$
18 Geo Jerry Osborne Schoon$^{r}$ Hampton from Piscatuqua
Misses Nancy & Mary Harvey belong$^{g}$ to Boston
Joshua Hall Sloop Ranger from N Carolina
M$^{r}$ John Bonner, M$^{r}$ Matthew Scott — Merchts.
Hugh Hunter Ship Devonshire from London
Step$^{n}$ Sayres Esq$^{r}$ Merch$^{t}$
Cap$^{n}$ Geo Glover Cap$^{n}$ Archab Dunmore Marrin$^{rs}$
Madam Kan Sister to the late Doct Douglass
Madam Robison Daughter to Madam Ken
23 Geo. Brayley Brig Cato from Swansey
M$^{r}$ Reynolds a Gen$^{tm}$
26 Israel Abbott Sloop Polley from Connecticut
M$^{r}$ Pendicks Trader
30 W$^{m}$ Wimble Sloop Stamford from N. Y.
The Rev$^{d}$ M$^{r}$ Mears
M$^{r}$ Dickison a Merch$^{t}$
M$^{r}$ Searle Sister to M$^{r}$ Gore of Boston.
July 4 James Dickey Schoon$^{r}$ Free America from Anapolis
Sarah Bears Spinster
M$^{rs}$ Lansford a Widow
Joseph Starrett Farmer

Andrew Wilson Sloop Cecelia from Jamaica
Cap$^{n}$ Edward Tyler Marriner
M$^{r}$ Will$^{m}$ Hanson Merch$^{t}$
Andrew Gardner Brig$^{t}$ Swallow [from] Bristol
M$^{rs}$ Griffin & Maid
James Scott Brig$^{t}$ Lydia from London
M$^{r}$ Benj Gerrish }
M$^{r}$ Rob$^{t}$ Fletcher } Gentle$^{n}$
John Rose Shoemaker
W$^{m}$ Paty a Currier
George Betty Brazier & His Wife
7 Edward Howes. Schoon$^{r}$ Eliz$^{th}$ from Hallifax
Cap$^{n}$ Gwin
Cap$^{n}$ Beals & Son
John Demount Butcher His Wife & Mother
9 John Hooker Schoon$^{r}$ Abig$^{l}$ from Piscatuqua
Miss Mary Warner Spinster
M$^{rs}$ Libey Widow
12 Justus Taylor Sloop 3 partners from Connect$^{t}$
M$^{r}$ Creeke a Merch$^{t}$ His Wife & 4 children
Thom$^{s}$ Hopkins Sloop Cale from Connect$^{t}$
M$^{r}$ Cullam a Baker
Noah Doggett Sloop Commerce from N. Carolina
M$^{r}$ Thom$^{s}$ Gilbreth Merch$^{t}$
14 Will$^{m}$ Sherad Ship Brutus from S$^{th}$ Carolina
M$^{r}$ W$^{m}$ Warrien a Merch$^{t}$
Nathl. Atwood Sloop Swallow from Hallifax
M$^{r}$ Jam$^{s}$ Forrist Merch$^{t}$ & two Servants
Isaac Stone Trader & Serv$^{t}$
Mary Ingill Wife to a Carpenter at Hallifax
Eliz$^{th}$ Bridge Wife to a Founder & child
Sam$^{l}$ Vans }
Joshua French } Merch$^{ts}$.
Sherman Lewis Sloop Polly from Connecticut
Miss Charity Johnson }
Miss Easter Lampson } for Education.
Phineas Baldwin Sloop Fairfield [from] Connecticut
M$^{r}$ Mayhew a Gent$^{m}$
John Whitmarsh Scoon$^{r}$ Dove from Philadep$^{h}$
The Rev M$^{r}$ Kentow from Nova Scotia
M$^{r}$ Cha$^{s}$ Cameron a Trader
Mary Hardgrave Wife to a Stationer at Philadelphia & her Daughter
15 John Cathcart Ship Cicero from S. Carrolina
The list of Passengers not given in.
21 Jerem$^{h}$ Rogers Scoon$^{r}$ Nova Scotia Packet from Hallyfax
Cap$^{n}$ Allen a Marriner
Eliz$^{th}$ Cream a Spinster.
25 Moses Bennett Scoon$^{r}$ Peggy from Madera
Álvaro, de Ornellas, Narconallas Cysniris
Manuel de Morem. Two Portugese Gentlemen

James Ford Sloop Nancy from Hallyfax
Alex^r Frasier a Marriner
Ebn^r Wales a Trader
William —— a Labourer
26 Uriah Oakes Scoon^r Margaret from Louisbourg
Mary Stacker a girl to the care of M^rs Creamer
Patrick Dowling a Shoemaker
Edw^d Whealand a Fisherman
28 David Wier Scoon^r Rainbow from Quebec
Cap Benj Cobb a Marriner
Lawrence Gilchrist a Baker
Nath Patten Sloop Betty from N. Carrolina
M^r W^m Tyler, Killey } Merch^ts
M^r Mathew Richee }
M^r Munn a Hatter.
30 John Dean Brig Countess of Bute from Jamaica
M^r Mosses Alvares } Merch^ts
M^r Jacob Mindis }
Cap^n John Blow a Marriner
31 Isaac Phillips Sloop Nancy from N. Found Land
M^rs Dumeresque a Widow & her Daughter
Aug 1 Tim^th Parker Sloop three friends from Philadelp^a
M^r Lodwick Sprodell }
M^r Rob^t Gray } Merch^ts
M^r Duncan }
M^r Pelatiah Webster }
2 Thom^s Homer Sloop Rainbow from N. Carrolina
M^r John Coleman a Merch^t
Abiel Lucas Scoon^r Gloria from Canso
M^r Barnabas Fagen his wife & child
5 Josiah Goreham Sloop America from Philadelphia
Cap^n Joseph Arthur a Marriner
7 Will^m Hayman Schoon^r Lovely Betsey [from] Scotland
Cap^n Rob^t Service }
Cap^n M^cEvan } Marriners
Cap^n Rob^t Morrison His mate & Servt. }
Geo Hanshald Rob^t Gillies }
Jam^s Henderson Arthur Hamilton } Merch^ts
Alex^r Ferguson Rob^t Pludder }
M^r Thom^s Robertson & Wife for Annapolis Royal
M^r Brown for Ditto [Annapolis Royal]
Robert Thompson for New York.
Elisha Glover Schoon^r Charm^g & Hannah [from] Nova Scotia
John Jeffers Farmer & Wife
Joanna Howard Wife to a Farmer
Ann Brooks Wife to a Ditto & Child
Alex^r M^cGhune a Farmer
Jane Takels Wife to a Farmer
Dorkes Gallop a Widow
Sam^l M^cClentick a Lad for Education

10 Calvin Delano Sloop Hannah [from] North Carolina
Jacob Roberts Oterway Burnes Merchts
James Scott Brigt Ann from Louisburgh
Capn James Moor His Wife & 4 servants
Mr James Morrison a Leuvt
13 Paschal Nelson Smith Sloop Speedwell from N. York
Lieut Peirce & Lady
Capn Rogers of the Rangers
Capn Heath a Marriner
19 Alden Bass Sloop Speedwell from Barbadose
Doct Edward Bancroft
Cap Edmd Wanton a Marriner
20 Jacob Cole Brig Juno from N. F. Land
John Lambert, Charles S Penn — Marriners
Patrick Poor Carpenter
22 Wm Deverson Junr Ship Tho & Sam from Quebec
Cap Lewis Fits Gerrald
25 Joshua Shaw Scoonr Priscilla from Hallyfax
Cap Cotnam of Salem & a Nurse wth a child of his Daughters
Joshua French & Terrell Owen Traders
Josiah Rogers Scoonr Eliz from Philada
Capn Robert Way a Marriner
26 George Haskins Sloop Brittania from Nantucket
Miss Ruth Hoskins Spinster
Miss Matha Dexter Ditto.
Jeremh Rogers Schoonr Nova Scotia [from] Hallifax
27 Mr John Apthorp, Mr Benjn Jackson — Merchts
Mrs Salter Her Child & Servt
Mrs Franklin 2 children & Servt.
Sept 2 Zebulen Elliot Sloop Greyhound [from] Connecticut
William Brocas a Merch't
John McGregor Sloop Endeavr from Annapolis
Sarah Rice a Spinster
6 Timth Parker Sloop 3 Friends [from] Philadelphia
Mr Corns Linsey a Gentleman
John Wood a Sailor
8 Jonth Freeman Ship Pratt from London
Mr Heny Bromfield, Mr Gilbert Deblois, Mr John Pinchbank, Mr Sam Parker — Merchants.
Mr Fras Brezina a German
13 John Banfield Brigt Thomas from Guadalop & St Eustatia
Mr Benjn Bunting Mercht
Mr Kno. Mr Marroie French Gentlemen
15 Heny Omand Ship Generl Wolf from London
Mr Edward Church, Mercht Mr Rob Silkreg Ditto
Capn Thomms Carlett Marriner

Miss Hannah Wilkinson Spinster
Cap[n] Tho[s] Deads a Marriner His wife & child
Thom[s] Omand, Joseph Smith & Jam[s] Smith Marriners
Thom[s] Carmichall a Weaver
Allen Muris Merch[t] Peter Hagan a Taylor
Patrick Naster Soap Boiler Char[s] Fenton Farmer
Benj[n]. Gorstelow a Soap Boiler
John Gould Merch[t] Thos Wells Taylor
Cap[n] Rob[t] Stone of His Town
Cap[n] Hen[y] Willson Marriner & servant
Joseph Pell Shoemaker His Wife & 2 children

Sept 6 Josiah Gorham Sloop America from Philadelphia
John Moor Merch[t] & 3 Sailors

17 Sam[l] Bragdon Sloop Sybella from S[th] Carolina
John Gange Taylor
John Homer Cooper

John Hogsdon Sloop Prince of Orange [from] Burmuda
M[r] Shaw Blacksmith
M[r] Lewis Blockmaker
M[r] Daken Blacksmith
M[r] Pope Dancing Master.

18 Will[m] Marshall Ship Holy Oake from London.
Cap[n] James Brett Marriner
Cap[n] Tho[s] Tyler Ditto & serv[t]
M[r] Rider a Merch[t]
John Brown Soap Boyler His Wife & 2 Children
Thom[s] Broadbear Taylor
Will[m] Ferryman a Merch[ts] Clarke

John Pullen Schoon King Fisher from Louisburg
Cap[t]. Cesar Cormack of the Rangers
Mr. Joseph Simson Merch[t].

Nath[l] Atwood Sloop Swallow from Hallifax
John Terrey Baker
W[m] White Ditto & Son
John Rite a Leiut of one of His Majestys Ships & Serv[t]
M[r] Char[s] Rollen Merch[t]
M[rs] Weitten a Cooper Wife at Hallifax & Son
Cap[n] Shadwick in the Army
Char[s] Orston Docter
John Ray Merch[t]
2 Seamen.

19 Edward Morrison Schoon[r] Blackburn from Glasgow
John Neal, Sailor, Dav[d] Rening, Alex[r] Ramsay, W[m] Cockren, James Gellis, Sam[l] Spark. } Marriners
Joseph Service,

20 John Broad Brig[t] Fly from Falmouth
John Polkinham Christop Spurrier mates for a ship & 5 Sailors

21 Constant[e] Freeman Ship Juno [from] Bristol
M[r] John Powell Merch[t].

Sept 23 W$^{m}$ Deverson Ship Brittania from London
Cap$^{n}$ Jennings a Marriner
M$^{r}$ Bowen an Officer w$^{th}$ his Wife.
Rob$^{t}$ Buckan a Trader
W$^{m}$ Davis Ship Thomas from London
M$^{r}$ Rich$^{d}$ Barnssley a Gen$^{m}$ & his Wife
Cap Gallispie & Wife
Cap John Phillips & Mate.
Cap Jn$^{o}$ Parrott & Mate. } Marriners
Cap Jn$^{o}$ Darling & Do.
27 Jeremiah Rogers Scoon$^{r}$ Nova Scotia Packet from Hallyfax
M$^{r}$ Fra White a Mercht
Doc$^{r}$ White of Hallifax
Ruth Rogers
Dorcas Cleavland } Spinsters.
Eliz. Blackden
W$^{m}$ Clift Scoon$^{r}$ Two Sisters from Louisbourgh
Gregory Townsend Esq & 2 serv$^{ts}$
M$^{r}$ Hogg Master of a ship of warr at Hallifax
M$^{r}$ Despert Ensign
Joseph Blanchard Sloop Dolphin from N. Fd Land
Cap$^{n}$ Fran$^{s}$ Tree & Six Sailors
Cap$^{n}$ Cockran & 4 Ditto
Rich$^{d}$ Howell & Step$^{n}$ Nowter Marriners
Isasc Smith Sloop Bideford from N. F. Land
Cap W$^{m}$ Shippard & five Sailors
John Fanning & Will$^{m}$ Marriners
29 Eben$^{r}$ Rider Sloop Abigail from N. Found Land
George Chester, Thom$^{s}$ Sterling, W$^{m}$ Studman Marriners
Patrick Furnas, Edw$^{d}$ Casey,
John Latthorn, W$^{m}$ Scott,
Rodman Reed, Peter Rhine, } Fisherman
John Maragrine, Derby Morrison,
Martin McLartin, Edm$^{d}$ Butler,
John Killey.
John Anderson a Cooper.
Rob$^{t}$ McCurdy Brig William from Ireland
M$^{r}$ W$^{m}$ Moor Gentle$^{m}$. Dan$^{l}$ Boyles, Taylor & His Wife.
M$^{r}$ Barry, School Master. Mich$^{l}$ Poor, Labourer
John Feald, Jerem$^{h}$ Nuhan, Miles Cauly, Labourers
Tim$^{y}$ Shea, Patrick Roach Ditto.
W$^{m}$ Gorman, Weaver. Jerem$^{h}$ Murphy, Cooper
Jerem$^{h}$ Readon, George Fitzgaral, Labourers
John Kealahorn, Weaver. John Jenkins a Dyer
Sam$^{l}$ Allen Do. John Gray, Labourer
Sam$^{l}$ Dickson a Comber. Will$^{m}$ Hurley, Labourer
Tim$^{y}$ Dorson, Schoolmaster & Wife
Mary Butler a Widow & Daughter
Eloner Nowlan, Widow. David Stockman a Labourer

Andrw Chabrito a Sailor. Bryan Marran, Labourer Jams Meaglan Cooper & Wife James Wiley, Mason His wife & 2 Sisters. Thos Miller, Labourer His Wife & Son. Mary Wiley, Widow Betty Wiley & Jane Wiley Spinsters

Thos Duan, Labourer. Willm Scott School Master & wife

John Thumb, Saml Hanry, Robt Heanary, Labourers

Presl Pullen [?] wife to a Wheelwright & Son John Mealon Labourer

Jany Quales, Spinster. Grace Core Wife to a Farmer & 4 Children

Jacob Magar, Labourer, Robt Magar House Carpenter

Robt Main, Labourer. Andw Beard Blacksmith & 4 Children

Willm More, Sailor. John Fairservice Labourer

Jno Miller Blacksmith & Son

Betty Ramaige Wife to a Sailor. Jane Shanan Spinster Jane Patterson a Ditto. Michl Keanan Barber

Seth Doan Sloop Polly from Connecticut
Mary Starr Wife to Cap Starr of Boston & her Son.

Oct 3 Joseph Williams Sloop Polly from Nova Scotia.
Heny Higgins a Shoemaker
Experience Cross a Farmer
Lydia Hibber Wife to a Taylor
Priscilla Allyn a Spinster.

Josiah Rogers Schoonr Elizth from Philada

6 Larrance Ash Watchmaker ———]
Mrs Elizth Heft a Widow & Child

James Dickey Sloop Salley from Nova Scotia
Enoch Gooding Farmer His Wife & Two children
Moses Barnes a Ditto His Wife & Two children
Godfrey & Sarah Richardson children to ye care M. Wimens
Six French Fishermen Mathew Dulet a Tailor.

11 James Deming Schoonr Hannah from Connectt
Mr Garnsey Goldsmith & Wife

15 Phenix Frazier Sloop Salley from N. Carolina
John Frazur Peruke maker

Paschal N. Smith Sloop Speedwell from N. York
Major Bayard & His two white servts
Mrs Freeman

18 Moses Roach Brigt Squid from New Fd Land
Thos Whaland Saml White Coopers
Edwd Carey Thomas Roach
Edwd Griffen Luke McGray
John Mahan Thos Barrey
Richd Quirk Willm Comings } Sailors & Fishermen

22 Silas Atkins Schoonr Dolphen [from] New Fd Land
Capn Combs Marriner

Joshua French Sloop Fortune from Hallifax

Mr Stain Jams Bane }
Wm Finley Ebenr Thomson } Sailors
Nichl Bufford }
John Waterman Sloop Deborah [from] Philadelphia
John Pope Robt Gray Traders
John Woodman Gentlen

Oct 23 Jessee Harding Scoonr Success from the Island of Magillen
Mr Chafey a Brasier & Wife
James Bailey a Soldier his Wife & 3 Children
Ann Callehan a Widow & 2 Children
Sarah Sprague for Service

24 Uriah Oakes Sloop Success from N. F. Land & Louisbourgh
Morris Dayley Jams Casey }
John Newman Robt Wood } Fishermen
John Murrey Jams Sheppard }
James Cockran }
Mrs Margt Wife to Robt Wood.
Catharine Ormsby a Child to the care of Mr Gregory Townsend
Peter Crumer & Wm Brumigin Traders.

25 Cornelius Cannabal Sloop Gull from Liverpool in Nova Scotia.
James Nickerson James Eldridge } Fishermen
Daniel Nickerson }
Mrs Knowles Wife to Cornl Knowles
Percilla Mayho & Hannah Nickerson Spinsters.

27 Jacob Parker Sloop Dolphin [from] N. F. Land
John Barry Richard Rinch }
Wm Janison Wm Gray, Jas Kain } Marriners
Israel Turner Anthony Stodd. }
Robt Jarvis Brig Hanh from London
Mr Thoms Hutchinson Junr } Merchts
Mr Nathan Frasier. }
Capn Richd Small Cap Jno Langdon } Marriners
Cap John Haymer Cap Thos Hart. }

28 Alex Watt Ship Thames from London
Joseph Harrison Esqr Collector & his Family
Cap Benja White his Wife & Daughter
Mr Bowes a Merch
Cap Smith & Cap Clapp Marriners.

30 Robt Young Brig Neptune from London
Mrs Vibert Wife to an Officer at Hallifax

31 Archd Orr Snow Jeany from Glasgow
Mr Alexr Bell Mr John Miller } Merchts
Mr John Murray }
Mr John Fleming Printer
Daniel White Peter Ferguson
John McNutt Thoms Cockran
John Muire Robt Reside
Alex McDufie John Mcfee

Nov 1 Shubal Dunham Sloop Han[h] from R. Island
Mr Medcalf & Wife of Dedham
3 James Stuart Scoon[r] Nova Scotia Packet from Hallifax
M[rs] Fraces Camble & four Children
M[rs] Dunn a Widow
4 James Ford Sloop Nancy from Hallifax
Cap[t] Elisha Glover & 2 Sailors } Marriners
Cap[t] M[c]Cowen }
Eben[r] Wales a Trader
M[r] Fairbanks a Farmer
M[rs] Nancy Webb a Spinster
Barney Binney Ship Lyon from London
Cap Moldsworth of the 29 Regim[t] & Serv[t]
Cap Stowers } Marriners
Cap Hamond }
Lievt Johnson of one of his Maj[s] ships
M[rs] Ann Davis Widow & Daughter to the care of M[r] John Smith South End.
10 John Blake Ship John Galley from London
M[r] Benj[a] Berry & M[r] W[m] Cox Merch[ts]
Cap Sohier & Cap Hitch Marriners
Josiah Goreham Sloop America [from] Philadelph[a]
M[rs] Marg[t] Driskel a Widow
Cap Hen[y] Dawson Marriner.
John Whitmarsh Scoon[r] Dove from Philadelp[a].
M[r] Charles Camerin a Trader
Elisha White Sloop Trial from Connecticut
M[r] Berry a Merch[t].
Nehem[h] Soames Sloop Betsey from Hallifax
M[r] Kinlock a Clergyman
M[r] Miller & Mathew M[c]Namara — Traders
M[rs] Glover a Widow
M[rs] Clark Wife to a Farmer at Dorcester
11 Rob[t] Montgomrie Ship Geo & James from Glasgow
M[r] Andrew Donhun. M[r] James M[c]Master — Merch[ts]
Edm[d] Morton Scoon[r] Dove from Philadelphia.
The Rev[d] M[r] Williams his Wife seven Children & Serv[ts]
M[r] Beels a Marriner.
13 Shubal Coffin Brig Harrison [from] London
Cap Trail a Marriner.

15 John Harmon Scoon[r] Speedwell from S[t] Croix
Will[m] Hendrickson a Lad for Education to the Care of Cap Jon[th] Lord
Jon[th] Morcomb Brig Willmott from Cork

| | | |
|---|---|---|
| John Henderson | Catharine Sullivan | Jam[s] Coghlin |
| Mathias Brett | Marg[t] Ross | John Murphy |
| Luke Welch | John Gibson | Dennis Mahony |
| Mary Cockery | W[m] Quirk | Marg Mahony |
| Thom Dugale | Catharine Conner | John Hayes |

Joseph Mosses
Ann Dougale
Robt Dougale
Wm How
Justin Jeremh Davis
Thoms Dougale
Abig Dudley
Timth Bryant
Austin McCarty
Jonas Dougale
Davd Quirk
Wm Donshin
Ann Dougle
James Ross
John Ross
Janes Ross
John Ross Junr

Darby Lawler
Cathr Carrill
Danl Keefe
Mathew Howard
Thom Quinlan
John King
Chas Hewett
James Dalton
Cornelius Fox
Peter McNamara
Dennis McCarty
Danl Carthy
Patrick Welch
John Kelly
Barbary Kelly
Peter Manning
Arthur Veavea
Redmond Larnard
Cornelius Hagarty
Edmd Swaney

Edwd Murphy
John Twahy
Wm Stephens
James Row
Isabella Learman
Catherine Twahy
John Bourke
Patrick Ryan
John Bowler
Mary Dougle
Danl Bulkeley
Corns Sullivan
George Shinnehan
Wm Kahaven
Wm Fitzgerald
John Dowle
Bal Sullivan
Jams O Daniel
Thoms McCarty
John Lee

the above seventy two Servants are all Indented to Messr Creed & Collis Merchants.

22 Joseph Rose Sloop Industry from N. F Land
Capn Wm Cockeran
Cap Wm Bray
Daniel King
James Burn
Phillip Le Crais
Elias Le Siberrill
Peter Arive
Thoms Gallien
Jno Halloway
Isaac Wing
Archibald Tate
Cap Peter Hewson
Hugh Verncomb
James Clark
Richd Morisey
Thos Le Siberrel
Mosses Clement
Abrahm Podesters
Thos Allen
Robt Baswell
Wm Jones
Eben Hinkley
} Marriners

24 Nath Phillips Ship Dispatch from Liverpool
Cap Wm Main
Hector McNeil Sloop Fanny & Jeany from Quebeck
Cap Martin of the Train his Wife three Children & 5 Servants.
Lieut Willson
Mr Sherman a Soldier his Wife & Child

29 Joshua Shaw Scoonr Priscilla from Philadelphia
Sam Johnson a Carpenter & his Wife
Mr Robert Rogers a Trader
Isaac Smith Sloop Biddeford from Philadelphia
Mrs Ash Wife to a Watchmaker
Josiah Taylor Sloop Desire from Connecticut
Sam Knight a Sailor.

Dec 1 Joseph Dobel Sloop Charms Sally [from] N. F. Land
Cap Wm Clark a Marriner & his Servts
Mr John Mandervel a Land Surveyr

Dec 2 Wm Maxwell Sloop Sterling from St. Johns
Mr Jonth Whipple a Farmer & his Wife.
3 Isaac Phillips Brig Hawk from N. F. Land
Cap John Willson & Servt
Mr Thoms Kenady Mercht.
Mr. Thoms Kasey [?] Trader
Andrew Minton Joseph Stripton }
Jno Elson, Darby Rion, Wm Laurence } Marriners
6 Hugh McLean Sloop Nancy from Annapolis.
John Church Mr Moss }
Joseph Whillock } Farmers
Robt Black, John Cambell }
John Dennin } Soldiers
Mrs Martha Whillock a Widow
Lucy Rice. Nancy Kent Spinsters.
10 Ueremh Webber Sloop Lively [from] Philadelphia
Mr Robt Smith & Wife
James Dickey Sloop Sally from Annapolis
Doct John Wright his Wife & 4 Children
11 Rob Hale Ives Brig Unity from Bristoll
Mrs Margt Lilly a Spinster
Thomas Jarvis Sloop Desire from N. F. Land
Jno Haubury Jno Gleason }
Nath Linch Tho Fling }
Luke Dulin James Lase }
Morris Murphy Jesse Connelly } Fishermen
Phillip Dunelty [?] Thoms Power } & Sailors
Edwd Whalin Wm Murphy }
John Hade Pattr Brinnen }
John McDonnagh Jno Colston }
John Fling a Fisherman & his Wife
13 Wm Willson Scoonr Fisher from St. Johns
seven Fishermen belonging to this Province.
Mungo Mackay Brig Polly from Teneriff
Cap Darby a Marriner
John Andrews Sloop Massachusetts from St Croix
Mr Duncan Mackbun }
Mr Phillip McDunner } Planters
15 John Willson Brig Burnham from N. F. Land
List not given in.
17 Maurice Cavenaugh Scoonr Nova Scotia Packet from Hallifax
Cap Joseph Williams & Servt
Mr George Rumney }
Mr George Robertson } Merchts
Mr John Hall }
Joseph Dennis a Labourer
Mrs Margt Dunlap Wife to a Marriner
Mrs Eliz Cotter Wife to a Soldier in the Train of Artillery.
23 Nathaniel Atwood Sloop Swallow from Hallifax
Isaac Stone & John Wyman Farmers

Mich Carrell    Hen^y Noyce } Traders
Mr Beaver }
James Hilton    Lawrence Nutson } Marriners
John Miller }
Mr Spincer a Shoemaker.

Dec 26 Job Bradford Sloop Olive from N. Carolina
Mr Badcock Trader
Wm Dean Schoonr Thankfull from Hallifax
Danl Westcoat a Farmer
Andw Bright a Ditto
29 John Whitmarsh Schoonr Dove from Philadelpa
Mr Chars Gray Trader.
27 James Scott Brig Lydia from London
Cap Edwd Atkins a Marriner
Thoms Clark a Hatter
James Bruce Ship John & Sukey from London
Two Silversmiths
[Dup 29 John Whitmarsh Scoonr Dove from Philadelphia
Ent.] Mr Charles Gray a Trader
Sam Hooper Brig Phenix from London
Cap Cotton, Cap Brown Marriners

## 1767.

Jan 11 Nathan Sears Scoon Dolphin from Liverpool
Mr Malcom a Trader
13 Robt Calf Ship London Packet from London
Docr Richd Hirons
Nath Jackson Scoonr Phenix from Piscatiqua
Mr John Darby a Mason
14 Thoms Jenkins Scoonr Hanh from Hallifax
The List not given in.
— Thoms Dixey Brig Amherst from London
Cap Wm Grow }
Capt Termain } Marriners
Thoms Carewell }
Geo Davis }
20 James Ford Sloop Nancy from Halifax
John White Trader
Robt Kellwell Marriner
. . . . . Labourer
Nehemiah Somes Sloop Betsey from Hallifax
Maj Goreham his Wife a Child 2 Servts.
The Revd Mr Simon Moor
Doctr Bailey
Mr Hart a Trader
Messrs Ebene & Wm Wales Traders.

Mar 9 Uriah Oakes Sloop Sparrow from N. Carolina
Mr McConnel } Traders
Mr Mall }
Mr Teldin Marrinr
14 Maurice Cavenaugh Schoonr Nova Scotia Packet from Halifax

John Grant Esq a Gentleman & Servts
Mr John Gorham Ditto.
Mar 5 Nath Atwood Sloop Swallow from Hallifax
Brooks Watkins Esqr
17 Benajah Collins Scoonr Bilboa from New Liverpool
Benja Godfrey Trader
Tho Fish Marriner
Joshua Ford Blacksmith.
24 Joshua French Scoon Hanh from Hallifax
John Berry Trader
John White Marriner.
John Hart Trader.
Wm Derra Farmer.
25 Crowell Hatch Sloop Betsey from Maryland
Cap How a Marriner
30 Maurice Cavenaugh Scoon Nova Scotia Packet from Hallifax
Mary Rotch Wife to a Gardner in Boston and two Children.
31 Nehemh Somes Sloop Betsey from Hallifax
Mr Alexr Gray a Mercht
Mr Ebenr Wales } Traders
Mr Heny Gland }
Mr James Butler of Boston
Mr Saml Turner of Connecticut
Mr Saml Beffington of Nova Scotia.
April 7 Christopr Higgins Sloop Ruby from Connecticut
Cap Scott } Marriners.
Cap Ash }
Thoms Frasier Sloop Harrison from St Croix
Cap Benj Crocker } Marriners
Mr Smith }
8 Timth Parker Sloop 3 Friends from Philadelphia
Mr Woodbury & Mr Townsend Marriners
13 Joseph Cordis Sloop Ruby from Sth Carolina
Heny Fretts Saddler
15 Saml Adarton Schoonr Tryal from Connectt
3 Fishermen bound to Nova Scotia
Auther Wharfe Schoonr Industry [from] Maryland
John a Free Negro Sailor
Nathl Cook Sloop Delight from New York
Mrs Mary White a Widow
16 Nath Stone Sloop Molly from Philadelpa
Wm Henery a Tailor
James Fretts a Farmer
Wm Waters ship Minehead from Cadiz
Capt Hugh Stuart & Son.
John Marshall Ship Boston Packet from London
Mr Clement Jackson Mercht & Servt
Capt James Kirkwood } Marriners
Capt Phillip Bass }
Mr Lewis a Blockmaker

a Mollatto Serv$^{t}$ belonging to Cap$^{t}$ Whitman
April 18 And$^{w}$ Perkins Sloop Olive from Nevis
Mr Thom$^{s}$ Angier a Marriner
Jon$^{th}$ Pierpoint Brig Duke of Kingston from Granada
Mrs Abig$^{l}$ Jones Wife to a Marriner.
25 Maurice Cavenaugh Scoon$^{r}$ Nova Scotia Packet from Hallifax.
Mr John Munrow a Notary Publick.
Mr Thom$^{s}$ Morton a Marriner
Mr James Clapp a Cooper.
27 Alex Ramage Snow Concord from St Eustatia.
Mr John Dickenson a Carpenter
28 James Hall Ship Amazon from London
Cap$^{n}$ Alex Smith Marrin$^{r}$
Mr John Atkinson, Clarke to Mr Smith.
May 4 James Burton Schoon$^{r}$ Hannah [from] Nova Scotia
John Savage, John Gorley, Edw$^{d}$ Brooks } Farmers.
Mrs Eliz$^{th}$ Corbet Wife to a Farmer.
Tho$^{s}$ Elsbere Sloop Ranger from Rh$^{d}$ Island
Mrs Smith Wife to Cap$^{n}$ Smith
Gideon Dodge Cooper
Mr Turner House Carpenter
Mr Nich$^{s}$ Probery Trader.
5 W$^{m}$ Edwards Sloop Huldah from Connect$^{t}$
Char$^{s}$ Dupee His wife & 10 Children } bound to Quebec
Joseph —— His wife & Son }
7 Nath Atwood Sloop Nancy from Hallifax
Mr James Fudge a Merch$^{t}$
Edward Pell a Baker.
Mrs Mary —— & Child to the care of Mr Forist & two Dutchmen.
Hen$^{y}$ Oman Ship General Wolf from London
Mrs Esther Corney Wife to a Taylor
w$^{th}$ Two sons & 3 Daughters.
George Todd a Taylor.
Jon$^{th}$ Freeman Ship Pratt from London
Mr John Alcock
9 Thom$^{s}$ Debano Brig Union from London
Mr Jabez Bradley, David Stanwood, Rich$^{d}$ Mcdugall. } Marriners.
14 Jn$^{o}$ Smith Brig Squirrell from London
Mr Thom$^{s}$ Lee a Merch$^{t}$
W$^{m}$ Merth a Marriner.
17 Josiah Goreham Sloop America from Philadelphia
W$^{m}$ Price a Lad to the Care of Mr David Bell
20 John Midford Snow Apollo from Liverpool
George Ray a Butcher
Sarah —— a Servant to the Captain.

May 28 Edm^d Morton Scoon^r Dove from N. Carrolina
Mr Jacob Sheppard, Mr Nath Bowles, Mr Trisdale — Traders.
Wm a Coachman to Gov Winthworth.
Wm Maxwell Sloop Sterling from St Johns
Mrs Ralleff, Mrs Cockran — Wives to Soldiers at Hallifax
29 Richard Grinnell Sloop Industry from South Carolina
John Ward Serv^t to Cap Joshua Loring
John Dunn Ship Glasgow from Greenock.
Mr Arthur Hambleton a Merch^t
Mathew Limeburn a Farmer
John McKeller a Joiner
David Larmore, Wm Willson Marriners
30 Nath Phillips Ship Dispatch from Liverpool
Cap^n George Willson a Marrin^r.
Samuel Pain Sloop Commerce from Maryland
Mr James Stuart a Merch^t
Wm Fitch Scoon^r Three Brothers from S. Carrolina
Mr Lemuel Cox a Wheelwright.
Wm Welchman Snow Mary from Glasgow
Mr George Robinson, Mr John Lewis — Merch^ts
Cap John Loyle a Marriner
Wm McDuell Bookbinder
Mr John Delrumple an Ensign

| | |
|---|---|
| Alex^r McCordy | Wm Boyd |
| Gab^l Willson | Rob Hay |
| James Bryson | Alex^r McNaghton. |
| John McKillop | Mal^m McNaghton |
| George Sterling | Allan Scott |
| Thom^s McForland | Wm Brown |
| Dan McBrarn | Tho Sterling |
| Wm Willson | John Park |
| And Willson | Dan McVicker |
| John Craford | Alex McKendly |
| Wm McCracken | Rob. Leddell |
| Wm Mathew | John Anderson |
| Wm McGill | Arch^d Browning |
| John Gardiner | |

the above are Soldiers belonging to a Regiment at Quebec or Hallifax.

June 8 Maurice Cavenaugh Scoon^r Nova Scotia Packet from Hallifax
Mr Brenton a Lawyer his Wife & Serv^t
Mrs Smith Wife to a Merch^t at Hallifax & Serv^t
Cap^n Hollows in the 29^th Regimt & 3 Servts
Mr Sands Lieut in the 59 Regim^t
Mr Martin belonging to Lyn & Serv^t
10 John Adams Sloop Molly from St Eustatia
Mr Joseph Davis a Gentleman

Nehemiah Somes Sloop Ranger from Hallifax
Mr Jones a Merchant
Mrs Miller Wife to a Blockmaker at Hallifax.
A Soldier in the 29th Regimt
a Child to the Care of Bethw Kneeland
June 17 Thomas Davis Brig Poppett from N. F. Land
Cap Willson, Elijah Luce, David Dunkar, Daniel Thomas, Thoms Barrow, David Scuder, Daniel Mc Brine, Wm Fitchgeral, — Marriners
Joseph Chapman Sloop Dove from Nova Scotia
Collo Tong [?] of a Regimt at Hallifax
Daniel Jones Son to Deacon Jones.
19 Gershom Blin Sloop Under [?] from Connecticut.
Mr David Ellsworth a Farmer
David Bill apprentice to a Barber in Boston.
Josiah Goreham Sloop America from Philada
Mr James Tilfer a Trader
Paschal N. Smith Sloop Speedwell from N. York.
Cap Elijah Thacher & Servt
Wm Hall a Butcher his Wife & 2 Children
23 James McEwen Sloop Olive from N. Carrolina
Mr Wm Mitford belonging to Nova Scotia
Thom. Chandler a Carpenter.
Wm Cousins Sloop Eliza from St Croix
Mr Fras Creekee a Mercht
Mrs Eliz McKew & Sussh Thomas
to the care of Mr Creekee for Education.
25 Morgan Griffiths Ship Rialto from Bristoll
Mr John Jones a Mercht, John Duffy, Owen Carolina, Partrick Caroline, Jno Hand, Lawrence Merren, Carrick McRoss — Traders all from ye north of Ireland.
27 Seth Doan Sloop Sally from N. Carrolina
Mr Wm Maxwell
29 Sam Haynes Scoonr Sussanh from St Croix
Mrs Durant & Child.
Alex Willson Sloop Dispatch from Liverpool
Wm Cleaves
Jane Bruce & two Children
Phillip Kennett
Jean Charlag & one Child
Rob Kewen
Mary Walker & two Children
30 Nath Byfield Lydes Brig Harrison from London
Fras Barnard Esq Naval Officer
Mr Phillip Dumersque a Mercht
Mr Wintworth
Mr Young a Wine Cooper
James Dickey Sloop Sally from Fort Cumberland
Ebenr Gawne, Jno Wright, James Hastings — Farmers

Jemima Vose a Spinster
Samuel Rockwell Scoon Betsey from Connecticut
M^r Barratt a Taylor
M^r Williams a Shoemaker
July 1 Tim^o Parker Sloop Three Friends from Philadlp^a
Cap Pearson Jones
Cap Nath Marshall & two Sailors.
6 Nath Atwood Sloop Swallow from Hallifax
M^r Sam Davis M^r Ja^s Hart. } Traders
M^r James Fitchpatrick }
M^r Eben^r Torrey a Baker
Mary Ryan & Child belonging to Hallifax
Maurice Cavenaugh Scoon^r Nova Scotia Packet from Hallifax
M^r Robert Apthorp a Gen^m
M^r John Cummings a Ditto
M^r James Brett a Trader
M^rs Procter Wife to a Merch^t at Hallifax
July 7 Step^n Stinton Scoon^r Charm^g Peggy from Cape Fear.
John Hughs a Lad for Education.
10 Peter Boyd Sloop Patty from Connecticut
M^r Tim^th Ward a Goldsmith.
Nath Stone Sloop Molly from Philadelphia.
Cap Thom^s Cordis Sam Berry } Marriners
David Vickery }
11 Isaac Clark Sloop Virgin from N. Carrolina
M^r Hill a Planter.
14 Joshua Hall Sloop Ranger from N. Carrolina
Doct Will^m Pratt
M^r Crosby a Hatter
Thom^s Elsbree Sloop Ranger from R. Island
M^r Fra^s Hambilton a Merch^t & Wife
27 Christop^r Prince Brig Nassau from Georgia
Cap Skilling & his Wife.
29 John Doubleday Brig Mairmaid from Haneago
John Hollyoke a Cooper
Joseph Waterman Sloop Dolphin from N. Carolina
M^r Cooper a Trader
Cap Bosworth
30 Paschal N. Smith Sloop Speedwell from N. York
Jane Waters Wife to a Carp^r at N York
Aug 4^th Joseph Hewett Sloop Phenix from N. Carrolina
John Combes & W^m Angerson Traders
Eben^r Fuller Sloop Good Intent from N. Carrolina
M^r Mathew Scott & Jn^o Vines Merch^ts
Joseph Goodwin Schoon^r Johan^a from Providence
M^r Newell a Cooper
5 Alden Bass Sloop Sarah from Granada
M^r Nich Welch a Cooper
And^rw Johnson Schoon^r Susa^h from Connecticut
M^r Thomas Edwards a Jeweller
10 Hector McNeil Sloop Brittania from Quebec

Mr $W^{m}$ Minott a Merch
Peter Ducett a Marriner
—— Lawrence a Soap Boiler

Aug 11 Martin Cox Ship Weatherell from St Christopher
The $Rev^{d}$ Mr Clarkson of Nevis
Cap $Thom^{s}$ Yard
$M^{r}$ Pratt a Shipwright

12 George Michell Schooner Molly from Annapolis
Charles Bartux for Education
Eben Perry a Farmer his Wife & Two Children
$M^{rs}$ Isabella Morley Wife to a Farmer & Child
Lydia Shaw a Servt to $Cap^{t}$ Mitchell

13 John Hickling Brig William from N. F. Land
Capt John Hayward & 5 Sailors
$W^{m}$ Lawren a Marriner

14 $Eben^{r}$ Goodwin Schooner Mulbery from $N^{th}$ Carolina
$M^{r}$ $Jam^{s}$ Harding & Mr $W^{m}$ Gould a Merchant
Maurice Cavenaugh Schooner Nova Scotia Packet from Halifax
$M^{r}$ Jno Romney & Giles Tidmarsh Merchᵗ.
$M^{r}$ Jno Pagett Watchmaker. George Bailey Soap Boyler
$M^{r}$ Foster & Mr Avery of Boston Merchts.
Henry Gibbons a Soldier & his Wife
$M^{rs}$ Fairbanks & Child of Halifax
$M^{rs}$ Cottnam & Maid of Salem
James Burton Schooner Charming Hannah from Port Cumberland
$M^{r}$ Smith a $Merch^{t}$
$Eliz^{a}$ Smith of Boston.
$M^{rs}$ Gay of Stoughton.

17 John Dean Brig Ann from Jamaica.
$M^{r}$ $W^{m}$ Penny a $Merch^{t}$
$W^{m}$ Pease a Marriner
Hector Orr Snow Jeany from Glasgow
$M^{r}$ $W^{m}$ Pettegrew Mr $Jn^{o}$ Watson, $M^{r}$ $W^{m}$ Buckannan } Surgeons
$M^{r}$ Rob Selkrige Mr Donnald Morrison, $M^{r}$ Patrick $M^{c}$Masters — Mr Tho Buckenloss } $Merch^{ts}$
$Tho^{s}$ Deeds, Rob Hamilton, Donald $M^{c}$-Donnell, $W^{m}$ Flatt, John Abernathy } Marriners
Peter Campbell John $M^{c}$Intoch, John Robertson } House Carpenters
Daniel Morrison a Ditto & his Wife.
John Park a Mason his Wife & 3 Children
$M^{rs}$ Thompson & three Children
Pettergrow a Boy

27 Simeon Freeman Sloop Betsey from Connecticut
Moses Pierce & his Wife.

31 Lemuel Drew Scoon[r] Vigorus from New Liverpool
Joshua Ball a Labourer
John Goddard Sloop Kitty from N. Carolina
M[r] James Burt a Get[m]
Nehemiah Somes Sloop Ranger from Hallifax
M[r] Wicoff a Merch[t] belong[g] to Philadelphia
M[r] Cook a Marriner
M[r] Wales Mr Miller Traders
M[r] Salter a Carp[r]
M[rs] Bushnell of Hallifax & Child.
Polly Driver. Polly Pippen }
Rebecca Rogers. }
Betsey Stevens of Casco Bay.

Sep 10 John Stockdale Ship Brittan[a] from Jamaica
Raynes Barret Wait Esq. Gen[m]
Peter Richards Merch[t]

11 Philamon Winship Schoon[r] Grayhound
9 Sailors

14 Joseph Row Sloop Speedwell from Quebec
M[r] Patrick Mathew Osborne a School Master.

15 Edward Grow Schoon[r] Han[h] from Annapolis
M[rs] Evans } belonging to Annapolis.
M[rs] Baker }
Nath[l] Stone Sloop Molley from Philadelphia.
The Rev[d] Mr Geo Soller

16 And[w] Newell Brig Polley from St Kitts
M[r] James Apthorp & Wife.

23 Nathl. Atwood Sloop Nancy from Hallifax
Maj. Butler, a Serjent & his Sevr[t]
five men belonging to Philadelphia
Rob[t] Jervis Brig Hannah from London.
The Rev[d] Mr Beach
The Rev[d] Mr Badger.

25 Joseph Chapman Sloop Dove from Nova Scotia.
M[r] John Chapman a Merch[t]
M[rs] Eliz Doan Wife to a Farmer at Nova Scotia

28 W[m] Ruggles Sloop Han[h] from N. Found Land.
Cap Casneau & four Sailors
Cap M[c]Farland & three Sailors.

29 James Smith Snow Charm[g] Polly from N. London
Mrs Sally Hill & Mrs Betsey Demorsque Spinsters
Sam[l] Rockwell Sloop Molly from Connecticut
M[r] Silvester his Wife & one Child belong[g] to Sheepscott
W[m] Whitmore for Education.

Oct 1 W[m] Maroney Scoon[r] Experience [from] Turks Island
M[r] Gilbert Malcomb a Merch[t].

5 Enoch Taylor Sloop Han[h] from Philadelphia
M[r] Abraham Field a Farmer.

14 W[m] Alkin Brig Ann & Marg[t] from Ireland

these are all Servts:

| | |
|---|---|
| Eleanor Murphy. | Mary Wilkinson |
| Franis Hadnett | Eleanor Stoakes |
| Mary Mchoon. | Mary Ambrose |
| Eleanor McSweney | Mary O'Brien |
| Mary Howard. | Thoms Prichard. |
| John Kinney | John Jackson |
| Elizth Brien | Sam Prichard |
| Ann Collins | Margt Fleming |
| Judith Pop | Elizth Wilkinson |
| Edwd Dammarell | Honer Coveney |
| Mary Callahane | Edwd France |
| Eleanor Moloney | Ann Hill |
| Mary Conun | Mary Stoaks |
| Timothy Mulcahy | John Lyndsay } Weavers |
| George Prichard | |
| Paul Prichard | John Murphy, |
| Dinish McSweney | Wm Sweney } Laborers |
| James Conner | James Fitzgerrald } Laborers |
| Darby Conner | |

Wm Hoban — John Baker — Shoemakers
Timth Murphy, John Furch — Talyors.
Isaac Stoakes a Nailor. Richd Terutch — Joiner
Joseph King a Clockmaker. Edmd Shanohan, Cooper
The above are Servts
Capt George Gray & his Wife
Mr M— Bryn a Labourr
Mr Step Gazor a Clerk
Mr Dinish Rien a Taylor
Mr Wm Buck a Shoemaker
Mr Phillip O'Donel a Cooper.

Oct 16 Wm Deverson Ship Brittania from London
Mr Samuel Barrett Mercht.
17 Wm Davis Ship Thomas from London
Mr James Pratt a Farmer
James Hall, Ship Diana from London
Pardon Sheldon of Providence
19 Robt Calf Ship London Pacqt from London
Mr John Glover a Mercht
Mary Cole Wife to Edwd Cole Marrinr & Child.
Seth Doan Sloop Sally from N. Carrolina
Mr Wm Kilby Mercht
Nehemh Soames Sloop Ranger from Hallifax
Mr Blair Mercht
Mr Williams & Mr Daniels, Farmers.
20 James Scott Brig Lydia from London
Cap Cordis & Capt Helpman Marriners
21 James Deming Sloop Harlequin from Connecticut
Abigil Doble a Child of Capt John Doble's and a Maid of sd Dobles.
Maurice Caveneaugh Scoonr Nova Scotia Packet from Hallifax
Mrs Gray Wife to a Labourer & her Child.

Oct 23 Wm Nichols Brig Devonshire from Bristoll
Mr Jonth Lewis } Merchts
Mr Benja Jackson }
Cap Mathew Smith
28 Heny Smith Ship John from London
Cap Benj White } Marriners
Cap Twicross }
29 Josiah Goreham Sloop America from Philadelphia
Mrs Hanh Prest a Widow
Jonth Freeman Ship Pratt from London
John Cockle Esqr
Mr Wm Russell a Mercht
Mrs Hanh Fosdick went from Boston in Cap Jacobson
30 Thom Crandon Sloop North Britton from Philadelphia
Mich Grant a Marriner.
Levi Studson Brig Jama Packet from Jamaica
Mr Joseph Fitch a Mercht
Joseph Hudson Sloop Polly from Hallifax
Gregory Townsend Esq & a Boy to his Care
George Osborne a Mercht
Charles Hart, Eben Wales } Traders
Abner Craft }
William Kirby a Labourer
Nov 2 Edwd Grow Scoonr Hanh from Annapolis
Phineas Lovatt, Wm Reed } Farmers
Jeremh & Isaac Fosters }
Mary Farnsworth & Martha Wheelock Spinsters
Joseph Starrett [?] Scoonr Granvil from Annapolis
Mr Nelson a Farmer
Richd Malony a Soldier
Jeremh Howes Scoonr Success from the Island of Magdalen
Wm Poterfield a Fisherman his Wife & Child
Tho Green a Ditto & Wife
Mr Green a Ditto
——— a Shoemaker
5 John Pulling Scoonr King Fisher from Louisbourg
Mr Row a Mercht
7 Alexr Watts Ship Thames from London
Heny Hulton Esq a Commissioner
Wm Burch Esq a Ditto his Wife Son & Daughter with 3 Servants
Charles Paxton Esq a Ditto & Servant
Saml Venner Esq a Secretary his Wife & Son & one Servt
John Williams Esq Inspector General & 2 Servts
James Porter Esq a Comptroller
Robert Temple Esq
John Hincks Esq
James Curgenven }
Thos McDonogh } Clerks to the Secretary
Sam Loyde }

John Hudson Clerk to the Comptroller
W^m Wootton & W^m Wotton two Lads
Mich^l Darcy a Lame Boy
Nov 9 Joshua Shaw Scoon^r Priscilla from Philadelphia
M^r Sam^l Eldridge a Merch^t
10 Moses Roach Sloop Fanny & Jeany from N. F. Land
Cap Fossey & 4 Sailors
Cap Treefarthen & 4 Ditto
Thomas Wallis & Tim^th Flaharty Marriners
11 George Folger Brig Lucretia from London
M^r Phillip Robson a Gen^m
M^r John Short a Merch^t
David Wier Scoon Rainbow from Quebec
M^r Pirkins a GoldSmith
M^r Mallau a Waiter at Quebec
Thomas Sturgis Sloop Dolphin from Hallifax
M^r Nutting a Soap Boiler & his Wife
M^r Richardson a Butcher
18 John Harmon Brig Speedwell from St Croix
John Irving Esq
19 John Dunn Ship Glasgow from Glasgow
James Kelly a Merch^t
W^m Russell a Mason
W^m Sweetser Sloop Han^h from Philadelphia
Cap W^m Bean a Marrin^r
20 Christopher Hoskins Scoon^r Mary from Ess Quebo
M^r John Segus a Planter
Step^n Crowell Scoon^r Defiance from Philadelp^a
M^r Barrell a Sugar Baker
21 Prince Goreham Sloop Desire from Virginia
M^rs Rasin Wife to a Planter at Virginia
23 John Waterman Sloop Deborah from Philadelp^a
M^r Charles Cameron a Trader
Dec 4 Josiah Rogers Scoon^r Eliz from N. Found Land
Cap W^m Shippard & two Sailors
Henry Righthead a Marrin^r & his Brother a Lad
Rich^d Barnes a Carp^r Dan M^cHaney a Tailor
Jerem^h Kane a Fisherman
8 James Dickey Sloop Sally from Fort Cumberland
M^r Winsor Agur a Marriner
M^rs Lucy Danks a Spinster
11 James Burton Scoon^r Charm^s Han^h from Nova Scotia.
Coll Alex^r M^cNutt

| | | |
|---|---|---|
| David Cutting | Fra Blair | Farmers |
| W^m Blair | David Dickey | |
| John Aughterson | John Hadlock | |
| Sam^l Whippe | John Savage | |
| W^m M^cKeen | Sol^m Steele | |

Abner Brooks a Farmer & his Wife
Sarah Richardson Wife to a Farmer
Edw^d M^cDaniel a Labourer
Lucy Stevens Johan^h Howard Spinster.

Paschal N. Smith Sloop Speedwell from N. York
Elizth Edwards Wife to a Marriner at Casco Bay
Maurice Cavenaugh Scoonr Nova Scotia Packet from Hallifax
Mr Reeves a Gentm
Mr McMasters a Mercht
Mrs Moat Wife to Cap Moat
Mrs Hoyland Daughter of Mr Cordis
Samuel Brown Scoonr Betsey from Annapolis
Benoni Shaw a Farmer
Dec 15 Archd Laws Scoonr Hilsborough from Quebec
Capt John Malcom

**1768.**

Jan 4 Isaac McNeil Sloop Swallow from Quebec
Patrick Conner a Labourer
Mrs. Eliz. Decon Wife to a Schoolmaster & 3 Children.
James Ford Sloop Nancy from Hallifax
Mr Wootton Inspector General
Mr Henry Green a Mercht & his Servts
Mr Putnam Mr Hunter, Mr Secomb } Farmers
Mr Balden Mr Wallis, Mr Wyman } Traders
Christopr Wagner a Butcher
John Masters a Carpr
Mrs Mary Hunter, Mrs Mary Malcomb } Spinsters
11 Tho. Church Scoonr Leopard from Hallifax
Mr Gorham a Mercht.
21 Nathl Porter Sloop Industry from Georgia
Mr Stephn Whiting Junr, Mr Saml Elburt } Merchts
Mr Jones a Leather Dresser
25 Nehemh Soames Sloop Ranger from Hallifax
Mr Night & Mr Baker Farmers
Wm Cowdy a Fisherman
John Davis a Marrinr
Polly Parsons to the care of Mr Bowman
Feb 1 Ebenr Wales Sloop Sylvia from Hallifax
Capt John Malcom, John Hamlinton } Marriners
Phillip Peak a Carpr
Mercy Parker a Spinster
3 Maurice Cavenaugh Schoonr Nova Scotia Packet from Hallifax
Mrs Harbert an officers Lady at Louisburg
Mr Glynn a Trader.
7 James Harding Stevens Brig Abigl from London
Cap Jams Ball, Cap Tho Hart, Cap Heny Eve, Sam Roberts, Thos Cain, Thoms Biscomb. } Marriners

Lieut W$^{m}$ Haswell his Daugh$^{r}$ & Maid
Thom$^{s}$ Irvin Esq, Rich$^{d}$ Shervin a Sadler
Charles Perring a Joiner. Tho$^{s}$ Richards
John Kilbany a Farmer
Katharine Winch a Spinster

Feb 22 Seth Jenkins Brig Friendship from London
M$^{r}$ Thom$^{s}$ Williams a Merch$^{t}$
M$^{r}$ Rob$^{t}$ Mackerle [?] a Doctor
M$^{r}$ Savage an Officer in the Custom House & his Wife
Sam Hawkins a House Carp$^{t}$
Cap W$^{m}$ Broig, Cap Symms, Cap Kirkwood, Cap Loyde, M$^{r}$ Hooper, M$^{r}$ Bradford } Marriners.
M$^{r}$ Brown.

March 6 Isaiah Atkins Scoon$^{r}$ Friendship from Maryland
M$^{r}$ Rob$^{t}$ Colwell a Trader.

11 Barna$^{s}$ Binney Brig John from S$^{t}$ Eustatia.
M$^{r}$ W$^{m}$ Gardner a Merch$^{t}$

12 John Havens Sloop Defiance from Virginia
M$^{r}$ John Hozo. a Taylor

14 James Ford Sloop Nancy from Hallifax
M$^{r}$ Woodworth, Asa Chase, Daniel Hovey } Farmers
W$^{m}$ Lawler, Peter Griffen, Charles Hart, And$^{w}$ Wallace, Charles Hill, W$^{m}$ Christopher } Traders
M$^{r}$ Fran$^{s}$ Anthony a Gen$^{m}$ from Fyal
Emanuel Wait a Mill Wright
Daniel M$^{c}$Clester a House Carp$^{t}$
W$^{m}$ Smith Lawrence Nutson Marriner
John Neace a Taylor.

21 Abiel Lucas Sloop Brittania from N. Carrolina
M$^{r}$ Hinkley a Merch$^{t}$
Cap Brown

28 Levi Stutson Brig Jam$^{a}$ Packet from Jamaica
William Harris Esq a Planter.
Joseph Waterman Scoon$^{r}$ Industry from North Carrolina
M$^{r}$ Benj$^{a}$ Pamella a Merch$^{t}$
Nath$^{l}$ Stone Sloop Molly from Philadelp$^{a}$
M$^{r}$ Benj$^{a}$ Sharp a Marriner

29 Josiah Goreham Sloop America from Philadelphia
M$^{rs}$ Nations a Widow
M$^{rs}$ Rebecca Allen Wife to a Marriner

31 Eben$^{r}$ Wales Sloop Sylvia from Hallifax
Elias Willcock a Farmer
M$^{r}$ Shanks a Tanner & 4 Children
—— Sloan a Serv$^{t}$

April 5 W$^{m}$ Reed Scoon$^{r}$ Nova Scotia Packet from Hallifax
James Brenton Esq a Lawyer
M$^{r}$ Thomas Procter a Mercht

Mr Thomas Mellish a Genm
David Row a Fisherman
April 8 James Scott Brig Lydia from London.
Mr Wm Cazneau, Mr Cyrus Baldwin, Mr John Cunott. } Genm.
12 Paschal N. Smith Sloop Speedwell from N. York
Mr Edward Griffin
13 Thoms Goodspeed Sloop Desire from Connecticut
Mr Shippard a Barber
15 Thoms Dixey Brigt Amherst from London
Capt Bast, Capt Cotten } Marrinrs
Wm Rose a Taylor
Edwd Griffis a Ditto
John Barnard a Brazier
Jonthn Freeman Ship Pratt from London
Capt Wood a Marriner.
20 John Pinchon Schoonr Easter [from] St Croix
Capn Maly Newell Capn Abrahm Brown Marriners
Mr Mathw Fenwick a Mercht
23 Nath Phillips Ship Dispatch from Liverpool
Mrs Eliz Walker Wife to a Master of a Vessell
26 George Mitchel Scoonr Molly from Annapolis
Mrs Worster Wife to a Baker
27 Eben Goreham Scoonr Lucy from Turks Island
Cap Burton & two Marriners
29 Peter Humphrey Sloop Hampton from Monte Christi
Docr Harden.
May 5 Edmd Morton Scoonr Dove from N. Carrolina
Mr John Bendor a Genm his Wife & two young Women
Mr Jacob Shippard a Mercht
Mrs Eliz. Covell a Widow.
Nehemr Soames Sloop Ranger from Hallifax
Mr Chipman Mr Mich Brown, Mr Wm Blake. } Traders
Mrs Mary Cobb & Mrs Lucy Pomeroy Spinsters
Mrs Jennison Wife to a Man at Dorchester & 3 Children
Thomas Newall a Child of Mr Newells at Hallifax
7 Nathaniel Stone Sloop Molly from Philadelphia
Edward Taylor a Gardner
12 Robt Jarvis Brig Hanh from London
Mr Lisle
Mr John Nazro
Rev Mr Wheeler
Mr Jarvis a Joiner.
John Smith Brig Betsey from Greenock
Capn Wm Fulerton & 2 Sailors, Capn James Leith & 2 Ditto., Capn Heny Trail } Marriners
Mr Archd Willson a Mercht

James Ure a Shoemaker
May 16 Samuel Blin Sloop Diana from Connecticut
John Bell a Marriner.
Winsor Eager Sloop Peggy from Nova Scotia
George Wood a Doctor
Thomas Dixson an Officer in Coll Gorehams Comp^y
John Howard a Farmer his Wife & 4 Children
John Crawford a " " " " " "
Mathew Fowler a " " " " 6 "
W^m M^cClentick & James Gurley Farmers
Lucy Danks Wife to Mr Danks at Cumberland.
21 Rob. Calef Ship London Pack^t from London
Joshua Loring Esq
Rev^d Mr Oakeum
23 Rob^t Adamson Ship Two Brothers from Surrinam
M^r M^cNeal a Gen^m his Wife & 2 Children
John Goodwin Sloop Charm^g Molly from Connecticut
M^r Mitchell a Schoolmaster & his Wife
24 Joseph Rotch Brig Squirrell from London
Cap^t David Lindsey
26 Laz^s Cobb Brig Molly from Guadalop
M^r W^m Tilley a Merch^t.
28 John Dunn Ship Glasgow from Greenock
M^r. Arch^d Bowman } Weavers
John Gray Adam Beg } Weavers
James Ford Sloop Nancy from Hallifax
names not given } Frenchmen
28 W^m Brown Snow Betsey from Hallifax
Betsey Lawler a Child belonging to Hallifax
Thom^s Gray a Clerk to M^r Belcher.
31 Tim^th Parker Sloop Three Friends from Philadelphia
M^r Alex^r Hill jun a Merchant his Wife & Serv^t.
M^r Hanaway a Carp^t.
Sam Perkins Snow Neptune from Liverpool
Cap James Boyd & Jno Mackay Marriners
June 1 Daniel Corning Sloop Brittania from Connecticut
M^r Gillson a Marriner
M^r Benj^a Grissell a Cooper.
Hector Orr Snow Jeany from Glasgow
M^r David Gray } Merch^ts.
M^r Donald Munroe } Merch^ts.
M^r John Munroe } Merch^ts.
Cap George Smith, George Stuff } Marriners
James Parker, John Cumming } Marriners
John Hyndman, David Hall } Marriners
Rob^t McFarlan, W^m Tuil } Marriners
Thomas Smith, Will^m Smith a Boy } Marriners
Mathew Eimsburner a Farmer & his Wife
David Stuff [?] Finley Cameron
James Sterett John Semple
— James Hall Ship Diana from London

Mr Gilchrist a Officer going to Quebec
Mr. Lee | Mr Frasar } Merchts
George & David Penman
Mr Demison a Genn
Mr Eagleson a Clergyman
Cap Shippard | Cap Main } Marriners
Capt Casneau | Cap Ross
Mr McDaniel

June 7 Howard Jacobson Ship Boscawen from London
Mrs Hutton Wife to one of the Commrs
her Child & two Servts
Mrs Hutton her Sister
Mr. William Blair a Mercht
Mr James Burrow Comptr at Hallifax
Mr. James Bradford his Wife & one Child & Servt.
James Harrop a Lad to the care of Mr Thos Russell

7 Robert Kinnidy Snow Boston Packet from Bristoll
Capt Martin

8 Sam Demming Sloop Phenix [from] Connecticut
Mrs Hillman Wife to Capn Hillman Marriner
John Dean Brigt Ann Penney from Jamaica
Mr Timy Penney His Wife & 1 Child
Sam Adarson Sloop Eagle from Connecticut
3 Frenchmen their Wives & 3 Children bound to Quebec.

9 Paschal N. Smith Sloop Speedwell from N. York
Capn Boyde } Marriners
Mr Jno Mallone
Mr Griggs a Farmer
Mrs Sarah Tucker a Widow
John Finley a Lad to the care of Mr Blair
Alexr McLean Snow Concord from St. Christophers
Mr Patrick Dupee a Mercht
Thos Frazar Sloop Betsey from North Carolina
Mr John Elott a School-master

16 Mark Clark Sloop Sukey from N. Carrolina
Catharine Way a Servt to Mr Thos Jackson

18 Josiah Goreham Sloop America from Philadelphia
Mrs. McKennedy
Mrs Cample Widow
Patrick Han a Trader
Abrahm Pearly from New Jersey

21 John Henderson Ship Duke of Cumberland from Barbadose
Capt John Lee
Capt Allison

27 Jonth Harvey Junr Sloop Earl of Bute from St. Thomas
Cap Smallidge } Marriners
Capt Nash

July 1 Abrahm Bartlett Snow Industry from Monti Christi
Mr McDaniel a Mercht
Capt Jellings

July 4 James Brown Sloop Eliza from Dominica
Mr Ezek Lewis Jun a Mercht
5 Ebenr. Wales Scoonr Sussh from Hallifax
Simon Giffen a Tanner
Edward Ellsworth a Shoemaker
Mrs Bucker Wife to a Mercht at Hallifax
9 Nehema Ingersol Brig Maryland Packet from Jamaica
Mr John Miller a Mercht.
11 George Darricot Brig Nancy from Granado
Capt Joseph Adams a Marriner
Alex Landale Sloop Sally from Granado
Mr Coppell a Mercht
12 Wm Johnston Scoonr Lucy from Nevis
Capt Long a Marriner
David Wier Scoonr Rainbow from Quebec
Mr Peter Fanieuel a Mercht.
Timth Parker Sloop Three Friends from Philadelphia
Mr Wm Compton a Mercht.
20 Saml Adarton Sloop Eagle from Connecticut
Mr Tarbox a Farmer
John Waterman Servt to Capt Waterman
Saml Rockwell Sloop Charmg. Molly from Connecticut
Capt. Joseph a Frenchman
27 James Dickey Sloop Sally from Annapolis
Anthony Burk, James Carney } Farmers.
29 Prince Goreham Sloop Desire from Virginia
Capt Joseph Tucker Marriner.
Mr Cummings a Staymaker
Aug 1 Nehema Somes Sloop Ranger from Hallifax
Mr Irwen a Professor of Musick
2 Edmd Morton Sloop Nancy from St Croix.
Mr Hutchinson a Carpt
Mr Eastman a Cooper.
3 Robt Gray Scoonr Hopewell from So Carrolina
Wm Randall Esq.
10 Daniel Tuttle Sloop Industry from Georgia & Connecticut
Mr Wm Belcher a Mercht
Mr Wm Jones & Mr Goulding Planters
15 John Saunders Sloop Sally from Granada
Richd Wagley a Mason & his Wife
Wm McCartey a Marriner.
Jehabo Whitmore Sloop Mary from Connecticut
Mr Fenner a Taylor & his Wife
Joseph Emerson Sloop Hawk from So Carrolina
Mr Stillman a Shopkeeper
Sam Scottow a Barber
Mrs Cambrige wife to a Clothier
Capt Wormell a Marriner. Mr Cary

Aug 15 John Cushing Sloop Dolphin from N. Carrolina
M$^{r}$ Fra$^{s}$ Newby a Trader
16 Rob Ball Sloop Sally from N. F. Land
Cap Patten & 4 Sailors
Cap Sheldon & 4 Ditto
Sam Haynes Scoon$^{r}$ Betsey from Quebec
Cap Benj$^{a}$ Torrey
M$^{r}$ Larey a Labourer.
18 James Ford Sloop Nancy from Hallifax
M$^{r}$ And$^{w}$ Wallis M$^{r}$ Charles Hill.
M$^{r}$ Philip Tidmarsh } Traders
M$^{r}$ Church a Cooper
M$^{rs}$ Eliz Lotter Wife to a Painter
Daniel Turner Scoon$^{r}$ Hampton from N. F. Land
Mich White a Marriner
Paschal N. Smith Sloop Speedwell from N. York
M$^{rs}$ Shaw Wife to a Marriner at New York
24 Arnold Smith Scoon$^{r}$ Industry from St Thomas
Stephen Harrod a Marriner & his Wife.
25 Eben$^{r}$ Wales Scoon$^{r}$ Suss$^{h}$ from Hallifax
M$^{r}$ Charles Procter a Merch$^{t}$.
Hector M$^{c}$Neil Sloop Swallow from Quebec
Benj Bennoi his Wife & 2 Children
Mich Dugas, Edm$^{d}$ Dugas
John Dugas, Peter Daufatt } French Neutrals
26 Joshua Hall Sloop Ranger from N. Carrolina
Cap$^{t}$ Fuller a Marriner.
Benj Randal, Blacksmith
Jehab$^{d}$ Simpson, Joiner.
27 W$^{m}$ Lowther Sloop St Andrew from N. Carrolina
M$^{r}$ David King a Mercht
29 Walley Adams Sloop Gull from Connecticut
Mary Ridley a Widow
Hugh Morris Snow Catherine from Glasgow
M$^{r}$ John M$^{c}$Master
M$^{r}$ James Falls } Merchts
Alex Crouckshanks a Goldsmith.
Will$^{m}$ Latta a Joiner
Sallie M$^{c}$Cartie went from Boston.
Sept 9 Eleaz Callender Sloop Dobbs from N. Carrolina
M$^{r}$ Sam$^{l}$ Ash a Gen$^{m}$
Abner Stocking Sloop Windsor from Connecticut
M$^{r}$ Tho$^{s}$ Moseley a Physician
W$^{m}$ Robertson Ship Three Friends from Granada
John Melveill Esq his Wife & two Servt$^{s}$.
13 David M$^{c}$Leod Sloop Ann from Hispaniola
M$^{r}$ Peter Debadie a Gen$^{m}$
Sam Haynes Scoon$^{r}$ Suss$^{h}$ from St Croix
M$^{r}$ John Fletcher
M$^{r}$ Alex Gray } Merch$^{ts}$
Martin Cox Ship Weatherell from St Kitts

Mr Wm Pridee a Merchts
Sept 19 James Angus Sloop Polley from Windsor
Mrs Jane Brooks Wife to a Farmer & 7 Children
Miss Rachel Long
Wm Collen a Lad for Education.
James Bruce Ship Suckey from London
Capn Titus Salter, Capn Jno. Showers, Capn Wm Ducket Marriners
James Scott Brig Lydia from London
Mr Richd Shuchburgh a Genm
Mr James Stewart & Lady
Thankfull Hawes
Thomas Desson.
23 Wm Deverson Ship Brittania from London
Mr Rob Bryand a Genm
Mr John Hambleton a Weaver & his Wife
Mr Simon Stewart a Millwright & two Children.
Timth Parker Sloop Three Friends from Philadelphia
Mr James Hall a Mercht
Mr John Sibbell a Marriner
28 George Mitchell Scoonr Molly from Annapolis
G. Richeson a Farmer
William Wigger a Shoemaker
Jean Spurr, her Husband at Annapolis
Rebecca Kent a Spinster
30 Giles Hall jun Sloop Elizth from Connectt
Benjn Henshaw a Lad
Willm Barber Brig Fair Lady from Hannago
Mr Merrett a Mercht.
Thoms Davis Ship Thomas from London
The Rev M. Biles Mrs Jackson & Son.
Oct 4 Nehemh Somes Sloop Ranger from Hallifax
Mrs Secomb Wife to the Revd Mr Secomb
Mrs Blackdon a widow
Widow name unknown & Her son
Mrs Juhan Wife to a Musick Master & 3 Children
George Russell Ship Lovely Betsey from Dominica
Doct McKensey.
13 Wm Malcum Sloop Seaflower from Piscatiqua
Cap Alexr Willson his Wife & Child
15 Eliphalet Smith Scoonr Sally from Connecticut
Mr McAlpin a Mercht
Doan Snow Sloop Betsey from Philadelphia
Mr Nath Porter a Genm
Mark Ferren Mr Webster Marriners
Stepn Jenkins Brig Friendship from London
Cap Supply Clap Cap Peter Cowes
Mr Wm Collest a Genm
Edward Tyler Ship Mayler from Bristoll
John Chad a Clothier
Heny Smith a Farmer
Redman Kelling a Trader

Oct 21 Wm Oliver Ship Deep Bay from St Kitts
Mr Edward Jones a Genm
Mr John Rand a Mercht.
23 James Ford Sloop Nancy from Hallifax
Mrs Wootton Wife to the Inspector & 2 Children
Mess Wallis & Hill Traders.
24 Ebenr Wales Scoonr Susss from Hallifax
The Rev Mr Palmer His Wife & 3 Children with two Servt Maids.
Mr James Burroughs Compr at Hallifax
Mrs Reynolds of Hallifax
Elizth Clewly of Roxbury & Her cousin Elizth
Mr Woodbury a Farmer
Mr Trail & Mr Bodie Carpenters.
Sam Black Sloop Sencua from Hallifax
Wm Scott a Brewer George Bergman a Baker
Mrs Cleas & one Child Mrs McLean & Child } Wives to Sergeants
Mrs Clevin Mrs Ervin } Wives to Sergeants
Mrs Hull & Child Mrs Clark Wives to Corporals
Mary Cannon & 2 Children Mrs Jones } Wives to Soldiers
Mrs Gillcress & Child Mrs Follen & Child } Wives to Soldiers
Mrs Stringer & Child Jane Brown } Wives to Soldiers
Mrs Dark Wife to an Officer & 2 Children
27 James McEwen Brig Grizel from London
Mr James Silkreg a Mercht
Mr Church a Ditto and his Servt
Mr Elbert a Ditto
Capt Price & Servt. } Marriners
Capt Cushing } Marriners
Capt Deael } Marriners
Capt Burnet & his Wife
George Dasris a Carpr
29 John White Ship John from London
Mr Samuel Gibbs a Gentm & his Lady
Mr James Cook a Trader
31 Aaron Purbeck Sloop Lydia from Louisburgh
James Sheaff & Heny Mon Marriners
Nov 2 Wm Church Sloop Unity from Philadelphia
Mr Wm Wittington & his Wife.
Paschal N. Smith Sloop Speedwell from N York
Mr Robt Moor a Commissary to the Troops
Mr John Ramage a Genm
Abrahm Vanbiber Schoonr Salley from Maryland
Mr Thos Jones a Trader
10 Nathl Stones Sloop Molley from Philadelphia
Mr Josh Jemmison Farmer
Elisha Turner Schoonr Dolphen from New Fd. Land
Capn Nath Curtis Mr Jams Foss Marriners
11 John Ranton Schoonr Betsey from Hallifax
Felix McMean Trader

Juda M^c^Mean, Mary O'Bryan, Katherine Alcock, Margret Morse — Soldiers Wives
Patrick Toben Trader

Nov 14 Abrah^m^ Brown Brig Squid from New F. Land
John Terrey, John Tracy, Nich^s^ Whealan, Mich^l^ Conner, Mich^l^ Colman, Dan^l^ Connel, Edmund Maugher, Tho^s^ Coody, Mich^l^ Collins, Patrick Hamman, William Kemple, Jam^s^ Hammons, W^m^ Hascock, Will^m^ Buckley, Walter Flanen, James Magee, Samuel Johnson. — Fishermen

Benajah Collins Scoon^r^ Endeavour from Liverpool
Robt Stevenson, Dan^l^ Torrey, Tim^y^ Burback, James Cone — Traders.

James Angus Sloop Polley from Nova Scotia
W^m^ Willson, Edward Brocks, Farmers
Eliz^th^ Willson, Rachel Huckings, Christopher Stevens, Mary M^c^Knit — Farmers Wives

15 Josiah Gorham Sloop America from Philadelphia
Doct John Sparrowhawk.

21 William Moroney Schoon^r^ Two Friends from New F^d^. Land
Thom^s^ Wallace Dennis Kain, Fishermen

Daniel Turner Schoon Hampton N. F. Land
Edward Russell, John Westlake, Edw^d^ M^c^Carty, Jam^s^ Dunken, Edw^d^ Welsh, Jam^s^ Hickey, Edw^d^ Linch, Terence McCarty, Jam^s^ Deane, Thom^s^. Jorden — Fishermen

James Arnold Schoon^r^ Ann from New F. Land
List not given in.

28 John Dunn Ship Glasgow from Glasgow
M^r^ Hugh Henderson a Trader

Dec Sam Dashwood Brig Deep Bay from London
Cap^t^ M^c^Neil & Capt Lavender

Rob. Jarvis Brig Han^h^ from London
M^r^ Symmons a Silk dyer & Wife
Cap^t^ Haslop & Cap^t^ Clark.

3 Dan Ketchum Sloop Swallow from N. F. Land
Capt Elnathan Jones & six Sailors
Capt Palfrey Collins & 4 Sailors
M^r^. Sam^l^ Casten a Mercht.

5 Stevens Atwood Sloop Defiance from Hallifax
Daniel Hovey, John Follitt, Jessee Howard, W^m^ Herrington — Marriners
Mary Tyle Wife to Joseph Tyle a Fisherman
Abigail Loyde Wife to Simon Loyde a Soldier in the 29^th^ Regt.

Eliz. Chambers Wife to Jn° Chambers of the Train
Jane Eglon Wife to Joshua Eglen of the Train
Sarah Slatter Wife to W^m Slatter of the Train & two Children.

Dec 5 David Wier Scoon Rainbow from Quebec
John Burk Jno Hooper } Sailors
Benj. Hooper M. Menth }
W^m Sweetser Sloop Han^h from Philadelphia
M^r Canutt a Merch^t
M^r Brown a Young Lad
M^rs Price a Widow belonging to Casco Bay & her Daughter
Josiah Rogers Sloop Bideford from Philadelp^a
M^r All a Taylor.

10 George Hardwick Brig Friends Adventure from Dublin
M^r Edward Baily Ensign.
Jn° Greely Scoon^r Leopard from Hallifax
M^r Millett a Farmer & his Wife
M^r Thomas Lapa a Brewer
Phillip Pisant, Dan Hogan } Labourers
John Madock. }
M^rs Clark Wife to a Labourer at Dedham.

11 Nehemiah Somes Sloop Ranger from Hallifax
M^r. John Lee a Merch^t.
M^rs Betsey Cream & her Maid. } Spinsters
M^rs Han^h Lunt }
M^rs Boyer & three Children

13 Richard Mott Scoon^r Molly from Nova Scotia.
Hez^h King Jno Bent. } Farmers
Ezek^l Gardner }
M^r Hughs a Soldier
M^rs Cattom Wife to Cap^t Cattom
John & Fanny Richardson Children of
M^rs Hyde now at Cambridge
Isaac Phillips Scoon^r Hawk from N. F. Land.
John Dunfee James Nowland } Sailors
James Mahane John Dad. }

15 Hector M^cNeil Sloop Swallow from Quebec
Capt Watt, Jno White } Marriners
John Burroughs, }
Mathew Gambett Tobacconist
John Thompson a Survey^r
James Keith a Baker.

26 John Esterbrooks Scoon^r Katy from Falmouth
And^w Fletcher a Marriner
Phillip Burgin Sloop Lady Moor from N. York
John Dehany a Barber
Alex^r Sweeny Scoon Betsy & John from Hallifax
M^r Ness Ensign of the 14^th Regiment.
M^r Dalton serg^t M^r Yeats a Ditto
M^r Kinney & Murphy Corporals

| | | | |
|---|---|---|---|
| Willson | Fanner | Yeats | All Soldiers |
| Killson | Bridges | Hibbard | |
| Eagles | Hines | Addsson | |
| Thompson | Sterns | Collens | |
| Old Field | Jepson | Comners | |
| Donagher | Clark | Cammeron | |
| Stutts | Sarkey | Marchan | |
| Dunbar | Thomas | Carty | |
| Grant | Somervel | Tyson | |
| Stevenson | Hengwood. | Walker | |

M^r^ Deed & M^r^ Cormack.

| | | |
|---|---|---|
| Marshom | Mattax | All Soldiers |
| Mardson | Kendrick | |
| Witherby | Westmorland | |
| Hollis | Ward | |
| Davis | Carlen | |

M^rs^ Hallman & Twenty Women with Ten Children.

**1769.**

Jan 16 Joseph Collins Sloop Defiance from Halifax
Eleakin Ross, Peter Glinden, And^w^ Wallis, Moses Hart } Traiders
John Larkin Jno Wootle Farmers

20 Thom^s^ Rogers Sloop Polly from Hallifax
M^r^ Peter M^c^Knap a Shoemaker his Wife two Children & 4 Servants.
M^r^ James New a Ditto his Wife & 6 Children
M^r^ Davededs, M^r^ Sam Armott } Gentl^m^ belonging to Philadelphia
M^r^ Sam Hasen a Trader
M^r^ Truleven a Merch^t^.
M^r^ D. Wolfe of Connecticut
M^r^ Paget a Watchmaker
Mich Toben, Thomas Walen, James Flin. } Marriners

17 James Scott Ship Boston Packett from London
Capt Jno Langdon, Capt Nath^l^ Sherburn
Cap^t^ Tho^s^ Hart

Feb 22 Sam. Pepper Sloop Speedwell from Hallifax
M^r^ White & M^r^ James Holeborn Merchts
M^r^ John White a Trader
M^r^ George Hewes a Butcher & his Son
M^r^ Carter Gen^m^
M^r^ Giffen, Dan Amesbury, John Huet } Farmers
M^rs^ Marston Wife to Mr Marston of Hallifax & four Children
M^r^ Samuel Morris a Survey^r^
Johan^a^ Whitcomb a Spinster

Thomas Hulme Ship John Galley from London
M^r^ John Bell a Merch^t^.

24 John Gray Brig John from Liverpool
Capt Creen a Marriner.
Mar 9 Phillip Conway Sloop Nancy from Georgia
Capt John Snilling
Alex Inglish Brig Betsey from Turks Island.
Capt Rouse a Marriner
13 John Munro Sloop Lady Moore from N. York
Mr Timth Seandal
Mrs Eleanor Bradley Wife to a Shoemaker
16 Saml Snow Sloop Salley from N. Carrolina
Mr Robt Duncan a Mercht
Capt George Cornell
20 Mark Clark Sloop Sukey from N. Carrolina
Capt Nath Blynn
Elijah Dyer Scoonr Rebecca from Maryland
Mr James Smith a Genn
23 James Dunning Sloop Cynthia from Hallifax
Mr John Savage a Trader
Robt Mercier Archd Phiney, Mathw Coleman } Soldiers in the 64th Regt.
28 Stephen Atwood Sloop Nancy from Hallifax
Mr John Avery a Mercht
Joseph Slowman Walter Brenock, Mich Brown } Traders
John Maud Taylor
Wm Clinston a Drum Major of the 29th Regt.
Mrs Willouby Wife to Ensign Willouby
Mrs Swiney Wife to Cap Alex Swiney a Marriner
April 1 Thoms Elsbre Sloop Ranger from R. Island
Capt Thoms Langdon
4 Wm Waters Sloop Sea Gull from Maryland
Mr John Witherhead a Mercht.
5 Moses Peirce Sloop Dispatch from Connecticut
John Warner Jackson a Marriner
Josiah Goreham Sloop America from Philadelphia
Mr Jonth Phillips a Mercht & his Wife
Mrs Crane a Widow
10 Joseph Hudson Sloop Dolphin from N. Carrolina
Mr Benjn Parmele a Mercht.
John Johnson Sloop Lydia from R. Island
Nathan Miller a Lad for the Printing business
11 Isaac Cazneau Sloop Betsey from London
Capt Edwd Stone a Marriner.
14 John Waterman Sloop Deborah from Philadelphia
Mrs Hensey Wife to a Fisherman
that Lives at Newbury Port.
John Skimmer Brig Nancy from Bristoll
Capt James Hovey & Alex Hodgson Marriners
John Raman a Farmer
18 John Briant Brig Wolf from London
Mr Walter Barrell a Mercht.
Capt Charles Ackworth.

April 19 Samuel Sweet Sloop Diamond from Philadelphia
Mr William Harris a Mercht.
Robt Calf Ship London Packt from Philadelphia
Mr John Russell Spence & Lady
Capt Heny Oman
Lieut Sinhouse belonging to the Romney.
21 James Tradwell Scoonr Sally from Connecticut
Mr Willson a Caulker
Oliver Johannett a Lad
Mrs Penniman a Widow
25 Zorobabel Slater Sloop Batchelor from Philadelphia
Mr Donerun a Genm & his Wife
Ebenr Goreham Sloop Molley from Georgia
Capt Isaac McDaniel
May 1 Saml Laba Sloop Success from Hallifax.
Mr Thos Boutineau & Mr John Hunt Merchts
Mr Saml Morris a Gentlm. Revd Mr Wm Moor
Mr Thos Marston a Boat Builder
Mr John Torrey a Baker
Richd Wood a Marriner
Mrs Peggy Tarlaven Wife to Charles Tarlaven at Hallifax
Jams Moody Ship Nancy from Glasgo.
Mr Hugh Gallaway Mercht.
Mr John Cambell a Ditto
Mr Andw Limeburner a Farmer
Paschal N. Smith Sloop Speedwell from N. York
Mr Mattin
Wm Hurl
Hannah Dwier
10 Daniel Olds Scoonr Polly from Connecticut
Mr Richardson a Potter
12 Edmd Morton Jun Scoonr Dove from N. Carrolina
Mr Jacob Shippard a Mercht
Mr John Payson a Farmer
16 John Smith Sloop Purchase from Connecticut
Mr Brodwell, Mr Cook } Farmers going to
Mr Cooper, Mr Honefield } Nova Scotia.
22 Josiah Goreham Sloop America from Philadelphia
Mrs Bray Wife to Mr Bray of Philadelphia & her Daughter
Uriah Oakes Sloop Phenix from St. Augustine
Mr. Davidson a Mercht
23 Daniel Messervey Scoonr Molly from Jersey
Mr Stevens Dumersq
Capt Joseph Luce a Marriner
John Barton a Farmer
George Caul a Weaver
Wm Le Bourden Chas Le Bourdon
John Le Grand Amice Grandin
Eliz. Grandin.

| | | | |
|---|---|---|---|
| Tho. Bingham | Joseph Boucher | | |
| John Dumersq | Cha. Colcombe | | |
| Amice Grandin | Dan Bessin | | |
| Phillip Gruchy | Clem[t] Gunnll | | |
| George Hammon | Ph. Grautt | | |
| John Gallikan | John Bourbonel | | |
| W[m] Le Roy | Jas Le Roy | | |
| Elias Watton | John Blovel | All Servants | |
| Jos Carell | Pet. Pinel | | |
| Cha[s] Le Masservier | Jo Jenne | | |
| Jo Pervier | P. Penny | | |
| Ph. De St Croix | Fra. Le Roy | | |
| Jane Fontenay | Magdalain Wie | | |
| Judith Le Roy | Ann Scobal | | |

May 25 Sam[l] Chase Ship Will[m] from South Carrolina
Mr Mitchel a Farmer
Abigail Emes a Spinster

27 Ichabod Stoddard Scoon Barsheba from Annapolis
Mr John Smith a Farmer his Wife & two Children
Mr Forsett a Shoemaker his Wife & one Child
Mr Tim[th] Richerson a Shoemaker his Wife & three Children

June 1 James Burtin Sloop Jolly Sailor from Nova Scotia
Gershom Leshon a Farmer
Sarah Fowler Wife to a Farmer at Brantry
Winsor Eager Scoon[r] Molly from Nova Scotia
Heze[h]. Egerton a Farmer his Wife & 4 Children
James Takels a Farmer
Betty & Nancy Corbetts } Spinsters
Mary Takells }

2 John Snelling Scoonr Two Friends from N. Fd Ld.
Mr Sam[l] Ware a Gen[n]
Robert Lewis Sloop Ranger from R. Island
Edward Hill a Barber.
Sam Rockwell Sloop Charmg Molly from Connecticut
Han[h] Blake a Spinster
John Dunn Ship Glasgow from Greenock
Lord M'Farlin & Son
Mr And[w] Johnston } Merchts.
Mr Rob Servise }

10 James Hall Brig Paoli from London
Doc[t] Jeffeirs
Capt Edm[d] Wendell
Mr Peter Vestaly a Merch[t]
R[ev] Mr John Clark

12 Davis Hatch Sloop Betsey from Connecticut
Mr Caldwell & Mr Hoskins Farmers.

14 Nehem[h] Soames Scoon Massach[ts] No 92 from Hallifax
Mr Robt Blair & Mr Jno Chipman Merchts.
Mr John Maud, Taylor his Wife & 4 Children
Mr Minot Taylor & Wife
Mrs Glinton Wife to the Drum Major

Mrs Loring a Widow woman
Mrs Foster & Child
Mrs Spring Wife to a Carpr
Mrs Sloan Wife to a Soldier & 2 children
A Lad to the care of Mrs Butler of Boston
A Girl to the Care of Mr Holton the Inspector
Saml Avary Sloop Windsor from Nova Scotia
Mr Wm Broodwell & Mr Jno Cook Farmers
Saml Skinner a Marriner
June 16 Robt Earle Sloop Betsey from Hallifax
Mrs Millwood Wife to a Blockmaker at Hallifax
Joseph Chapman Sloop Molly from Philadelphia
Mr Wm Gourty a Mercht.
19 Ezek Hatch Scoon Eliz from N. F Land
Capt Wastcoat & two Sailors Marriners
26 James H. Stevens Brig Abigail from Jamaica
Mr Patrick Briant a Labourer
Step. Atwood Sloop Nancy from Hallifax
Mr Hootton Inspector & his Servts
Mr Ansley a Collector at Quebec
Mr Bent [?] a Mercht
Mrs Pike Wife to Mr Pike at Hallifax
27 Joseph Goodwin Scoonr Johana from N. Providence
A Man & his Wife Servts to Govr Shirley
Peter Boyd Sloop Polly from Connecticut
Peter Vejostru [?] a Weaver
Mark Clark Scoonr Defiance from N. Providence
Mr Ebenr Love a Mercht
July 3 Saml Waters Scoonr Benja from Cape Nicola
Mr Martin a Mercht.
5 Sam Laha Sloop Ranger from Hallifax
Mrs Newall & her Child of Hallifax
6 Paschal N. Smith Sloop Speedwell from N York.
The Rev Mr James Greaton his Wife & Son
Major Robert Rogers & Servt.
Leiut Wm Peirce Royal Artilery
Capt John Hilton
Amos Breed a Shoemaker
Elijah Peck a Lad
Mary White & her Child.
13 Nath Patten Brig Dolphin from Jamaica
Mr Heny Askins a Mercht
Mrs Cross a Sailor
31 Daniel Howes Scoonr Sally from Annapolis
John Henderson Esq a Mercht & two Servts
Aug 1 Howard Jacobson Ship Boscawen from London
John Fisher Esq Collector of the Port at Salem & his two Servts
John Sober Esq his Lady, three Children & 4 Sevts
Cap Sam Lessely & Mr Sam Gordon a Trader
Elijah Luce Sloop Molly from Philadelpa.
Capt John Hickling & his Mate

M^rs Han^h Grace Wife to a Seaman at Philadelphia
Rob^t Jarvis Brig Hannah from London
M^r Ward Hallowell a Mercht.
M^r Tompson a Brasier his Wife & 2 Children
M^r Eggleston a Gen^m
——————— a Cabbinett Maker
David Stover Sloop Seaflower from Piscatiqua.
M^rs Gerrish a Spinster
Aug 4 Paul Junkins Scoonr Fox from Quebec
Jotham Gay Esq^r
M^r Thom^s Payson a Mercht & his Child
Mary Malcom Wife to Jn^o Malcom & 3 Children
five French Neutrals.
7 Nehem^h Somes Scoon^r Massachusetts Ninety two from Hallifax
Capt Isaac Foster.
M^r Benj Hurd a Silver Smith
M^rs Weal [or Wiat] ? a Widow
Benj^a Goulsby a Trader
M^r Smith
Jacob Hipper a Taylor & his Wife
M^r Ross a Farmer
John Walker a Coachman
Abner Stocking Sloop Windsor from Connecticut
M^rs Willson Wife to M^r Willson a Waiter.
James Robert Scoon^r Betsey from N. Carrolina
Sam Cornall Esq a Merch^t his Wife & two Daughters
Martyn Howard Esq his Daughter & Servts
Eliz^th Diamond a Spinster
Joseph Hurd Sloop Dolphin from Connecticut
M^r Peirce a Sail Maker
Francis Appleton a Lad
M^r Simpson
10 Robert Croell Sloop Jerusalem from Nova Scotia
W^m Scott & Isaac Farrar Farmers.
M^r Miller & M^r Smith
Thom^s Faulinton a Farmer
M^rs Camp a Widow & Daughter
M^rs Blanchard belonging to Nova Scotia.
14 Josiah Goreham Sloop America from Philadelphia
John Keats a Marriner
Catherine Alexander wife to Thomas Alexander of Boston
Abigail Brown a Spinster
Windsor Eager Scoonr Molly from Annapolis
14 Soldiers belonging to the 29^th Reg^t.

James Russell
Richard Russell
*Commissioners.*

INDEX

CPSIA information can be obtained at www.ICGtesting.com
Printed in the USA
BVOW09s1701261014

372281BV00009B/139/P

9 780806 305417